THE GIFT OF BELONGING

The Gift of Belonging

Johnni Johnson

BROADMAN PRESS / NASHVILLE, TENNESSEE

© Copyright, 1975 • BROADMAN PRESS
All rights reserved
4263-05
ISBN: 0-8054-6305-4

Dewey Decimal Classification: B
Library of Congress Catalog Card Number: 75-540
Printed in the United States of America

PREFACE

Another missionary biography? Not really. Rather, what follows is a brief account of the after-college years of Virginia Cobb, a Georgian who gave her life's energy to the Arab Middle East.

Virginia Cobb's story is unique because this unassuming young woman—thin, not too tall, of impish smile and penetrating eyes—willingly sought friendships with persons seemingly unable to open themselves to the Christian witness she lived to make. The story is all the more admirable because, in the last years of her life, she worked on in spite of a quiet, but losing, battle with cancer.

As time adds perspective, Virginia's approach to Christian witnessing may provide a model for many Christians. At the moment, five years after death, her servant life-style once again affirms qualities basic to Christian commitment, and also, the discipline and dedication essential to the everyday work of foreign missions. For Virginia Cobb was open to God. She looked beyond the routine of Mission committee responsibilities and assignments. She willingly accepted the group process, cumbersome as it can be at times. In it all she was able to recognize the freedom of a personal calling from God which she was to fulfill on the cutting edge of Christian-Muslim encounter.

She abandoned herself to the language and culture so diligently that the Lebanese frequently mistook her for a Beirut native. Dark-haired, of good humor and winsome, she fitted in; the people said she belonged. And, in fact, through most of 1967-1969 she lived among Muslims, lived love among them in the spirit of Jesus Christ.

Her missionary colleagues knew Virginia for who she was: patient to a fault, but capable of the sharp word; so gracious that no one, no matter of what opinion or station in life, ever felt belittled in her company; an idealist as concerns the gospel, but practical enough to move against national or missionary opinion where she was convinced principle was involved.

Many people have contributed to this writing. Missionaries, especially Nancie Wingo, Mabel Summers, Mrs. Jess Willmon, Mrs. Wayne Fuller, the Emmett Barneses, and the Paul S.C. Smiths. Also friends and colleagues, especially Mr. and Mrs. W. G. Cobb, Bassam Afeish, Dr. J. D. Hughey, Dr. T. B. Maston, Fon H. Scofield, Jr., and Dr. Jesse C. Fletcher who first suggested writing Virginia's story.

Indebtedness for all assistance, I gratefully acknowledge. Responsibility for its use, I accept with the prayer that in the ways God enables one Christ-follower to learn from another, we all may learn from Virginia Cobb.

JOHNNI JOHNSON

Richmond, Virginia

CONTENTS

INTRODUCTION

Tan Volkswagens are common on the streets of Beirut, Lebanon. Much more common—these VWs—than the conversation I was having with several missionaries as we drove from a Sunday afternoon Bible class.

It was June 1969. I was enroute to Teheran, Iran, to cover a missionary conference concerned with Christian witness in the Muslim world. That week I observed activities, and met people in a Christian school, a seminary, and a number of Baptist churches. Most of what I saw of the city itself was in going from one of these places to another. As we moved about in various groups and at mealtimes, we talked about Christian witness among Muslims.

Lebanon itself is not all of the "Muslim world," or even the heartland of the Arab Middle East. However, this half-Muslim, half-Christian nation mirrors much of how it is today. Here traditional faiths meet the city head-on. Here cultural mores are, most often, in conflict with the scientific outlook. Further, the capital city, Beirut, is a strategic transportations and communications hub for most of the world's Arabic-speaking population, and at least 100 million people in the world speak Arabic.

Driving from the Karantina (Beirut's "slummiest slum"), we talked about the city, its people, its sights, its charm. When someone mentioned its ghetto mentality, I was told how Beirut is divided into well-defined sections. The Muslim quarters, the Christian quarters, the Jewish quarters, the Karantina, and plush hotel row along the esplanade.

"You can't see them," said Virginia Cobb, one of the missionaries in the VW, "but walls really separate people here. High walls. For a person to cross the street from a Christian quarter of Beirut to a Muslim one is a longer trip than to China."

In the VW conversation we agreed that "Beirut-to-China" street crossings are a present-day phenomenon everywhere—in the Middle East, in South Africa, in the United States of America. Perhaps in less revolutionary times ethnic, racial, religious walls were inevitable. But today there is at least one difference: the street light has turned green. In every country, at every level of society, people of all persuasions are on the move. Some people miss the light in self-serving efforts to keep the walls standing but as the ferment continues, all the world's "Beirut-to-China" crossings are crowded.

The servants of Christ—Christians, bearers of the message that walls need not divide people—are concerned to cross all the streets that separate people from God's peace.

This is the kind of person Mary Virginia Cobb was. In her brief missionary career (1952-1970), she probed ways to cross the streets that divide the people of the Arab Middle East from one another and from

God's peace.

It puzzled her too that she often found Muslims more tolerant of Christians than Christians were of Muslims.

"This ought not to be," she insisted.

"If we Christians expect Muslims to listen to us, we must listen to them. If we expect them to admit our good points, we must admit theirs."

Concerned to bridge this gulf of misunderstanding, Virginia pushed her point.

"If you must argue about churches and the details of how a church works, forget it!

"We may need to sacrifice some of our nonessential emphases. Why start an argument about whether the Bible or the Koran is true? We can—we must—talk about Christ.

"We both believe God is supreme and deserves supreme allegiance. Let's emphasize that. Jesus did. Let's emphasize personal relationship with Christ. When he was here, he just said, 'Follow me.' They followed him. They watched him. They heard him teach. And then, after a while, he said, 'Now who do you think I am?' "

Virginia paused.

"Why can't we do this?"

Why?

With quiet determination, and the thoroughness born in prayed-over study, this attractive young woman pondered her own question. And she worked—the more purposefully as her Arabic studies led her into depths of Arab understanding experienced by few outsiders.

Patiently and steadfastly, in the face of frustration and sometimes opposition, she nudged Lebanese Christians, particularly Baptists, toward a new openness to their Muslim compatriots. By her own positive testimony and example, she encouraged individual Muslims to make a personal discovery of Jesus Christ.

During the years she served in Lebanon, she often functioned as the conscience of the Mission.* In lucid opinion papers, she questioned presuppositions about methods of Christian witness. She prodded the tendency of missionaries from America to impose stateside views on local churches overseas. She challenged the local congregations to deepen their concern for Muslims.

In her own approach to Muslims Virginia had one premise: "You do not win anyone without love because, first of all, the God to whom we would win *is* love. Our message is love, a distinctive kind of love; love that is unselfish. Unlike human love based on some return, God's love is the most powerful instrument, the only effective method toward those who differ from us, especially Muslims."

In evangelistic outreach, she pled for understanding: "When I love and respect and appreciate another

---

* "The Mission" refers to the organization of Southern Baptist missionaries in a given country. Virginia belonged to two missions: the Lebanon Mission, composed of all the Southern Baptist missionaries in Lebanon, and the Arab Baptist General Mission, the organization of those in Lebanon, Jordan, and Gaza—an arrangement particularly advantageous for publications, theological education, and broadcast ministries; since late 1970, unsettled conditions have made it necessary for the three missions to operate separately but now missionary-national committees handle interrelated matters.

person, I listen to him. I give utmost consideration to his opinions. And even if we differ, I try hard to see his point of view, to appreciate and applaud every iota of good I see in him. If he has faults, I lighten them as much as possible, see all the mitigating factors, and try to understand even these. I put the best possible interpretation on all his actions, attitudes, and words. I overlook the things he does that may offend or hurt me."

Living in this spirit, Virginia Cobb reached out to Muslims in the Arab Middle East. For many she opened a way to the Word. With a vision of the potential of the printed page, and "almost single-handedly"—to quote a fellow missionary—she initiated a correspondence course. She opened herself to the authentic dialogue of everyday life in the Muslim quarter of Beirut where she and several colleagues developed a public reading room and lending library. Her interest in education never lagged, but faced with a specific challenge she left the classroom to serve the Baptists of Lebanon and surrounding countries in the development of Christian literature. Then later, when a whole body of Christian education materials was available for Baptists, and other evangelical groups desiring it, she proposed that the church publications program be turned over to the national Baptist constituency for continuation on a self-sustaining basis.

In doing all that—and doing it in a way that won friends for Jesus Christ—Mary Virginia Cobb shared her faith among Muslims.

There were, of course, fellow missionaries. The missionary enterprise is, among other things, the using of each one's skills and abilities for the sake of the total witness. Finlay and Julia Graham, the first to Lebanon for Southern Baptists, made the initial contacts with evangelical Christians already in the country. James and Leola Ragland won wide respect in Beirut because of the Baptist school begun there in 1954. In the nervous years between Southern Baptists' Middle East beginnings and the Six Day War, the Paul Smiths, the W. O. Herns, and others worked with struggling congregations in Lebanon, Jordan, and Egypt. Among them, the missionary team worked to use all means possible in the service of the gospel. With these missionaries, and others, Virginia Cobb viewed her work as a sharing process. She gave her major energies to publication work in which, according to her successor, Missionary Frances (Mrs. J. Wayne) Fuller, she moved decisively, trusting that others would finish what she was unable to do.

Her death of cancer early in 1970, at age forty-three, took from our midst a humble, fruitful Christian called to serve God in the Arab Middle East. But her patient persistence—editing, encouraging, studying, changing when new evidence pointed to new approaches—pushed fellow Christians to look for God's green lights in Christian witness among Muslim people.

PART ONE

DECIDING DIRECTIONS

Each Christian needs to know what God's hope is for Christianity as a whole; and what each needs to find is to find the use God intends to make of him in fulfilling that hope.

W. O. CARVER

DECIDING DIRECTIONS

As soon as the formalities of college graduation were over, Virginia Cobb kept her appointment with the Bible Study Committee for the City of Reidsville, North Carolina, which had contacted her about teaching Bible in their public schools.

Yes, she told them, she was a Bible student. Her love for the Book, she dated from childhood memories of Bible stories and prayer at home.

No, she couldn't say that she intended to make a career of Bible teaching. At high school graduation she was set on being a research chemist. Time, and college, had changed all that. To be honest, though, she just wasn't sure.

"I want to work a few years to earn money for seminary. In the process I hope to discover what the Lord wants me to prepare for."

Her candor and qualifications impressed the committee. They decided that a Phi Beta Kappa with a major in Bible—the only woman in her class in the School of Religion at Duke University—was just right for Reidsville.

Two months that summer, 1948, Virginia worked as secretary in her home church. Then after a month's vacation trip to Canada, fishing and living outdoors on the Ottawa River, she traveled from her home in Statesboro, Georgia, to the new job in North Carolina.

Her pupils were first to eighth graders in four elementary schools, more than 1,300 in all. She learned that her predecessors in the job had each chosen a different course of study for the schools. Virginia submitted to her committee a curriculum outline to enable every child to have a balanced study of all parts of the Bible between the third and eighth grades. With committee approval of the outlines she prepared, Virginia put herself to work.

She was a teacher in the elementary grades but when she discovered there was no systematic Bible study plan for the high school, Virginia suggested a Bible club. Before she realized all the extra work involved, she had full responsibility for the high school Bible study club.

An employee of a committee related to all of the churches in Reidsville, Virginia, she was expected to visit the various congregations. She did, gladly and profitably. Frequently there were invitations to speak or teach in the churches. All the while, though, she was heavily involved in the worship and witness of one of the Baptist churches in the town.

Early in the year Virginia realized that a quiet dialogue was going on inside herself. The awareness was so positive that she came to feel God was using her work experiences to prepare her for—well, something else. In order to teach Bible, she had to study the Bible. This study led to serious prayer times. The study-prayer experience deepened Virginia's openness to God. Also she felt strengthened to meet classes every day and to accept the speaking invitations that came from the local churches.

Some of the invitations were from church missionary organizations. Speaking to these groups, or called on to teach "a mission study," Virginia realized she was out of touch with contemporary missions. In working through that Bible major in college, there had been less time for outside activities and the information she had previously got in GA studies. Trying to catch up, she widened her reading. She joined a new missionary circle being formed in her church. She even wondered if God was suggesting a course of action to her for her own future.

Reidsville was not all Bible classes in the schools and church activities. Her roommate was assistant director with the city recreation department. With her and the other girls where she lived—mostly teachers—there was always some plan in the making.

Then there were some of her school pupils. Like Joe, age eleven. His parents were divorced and he had few friends. His first visit to the teachers' house was not the last. In fact he came often, to get in on the Saturday morning painting sessions in the kitchen; no outstanding canvasses resulted, but there was time for friendship. Joe had questions about school work, and the way Christians try to live.

In the high school crowd, Kathy was a fellow Baptist who lived close by. One Sunday night, the first spring in Reidsville, as Kathy and her teacher walked home from church, a sudden rain shower forced them inside. They made it to Virginia's house and got to talking. About poetry. And life. Kathy told her teacher about a chorus she had learned from a retired missionary to India.

After the rain Kathy went on home, but Virginia found her mind stuck on the words "missionary from India." She went to bed thinking about them. All the next week, unbidden and when she least expected an interruption, the words intruded on her consciousness. For two weeks the experience persisted. Virginia prayed. She didn't know why she couldn't get the missionary idea out of her mind. Every time she sat down to study, there it was: India. When she prayed, one thing was foremost in her thoughts: India.

Virginia decided that she wasn't really averse to "this missionary thing." She just honestly did not know for sure. She was afraid. She did not want to make such a big commitment—or any life-determining commitment, really—without the sure sense that God was speaking to her.

School was almost over. She had a summer job waiting for her in Georgia. Monday afternoon, the last week in Reidsville that first year, she felt almost desperate to be rid of the heavy uncertainty.

Dear God, she prayed, *if you want me to be a missionary to India, please tell me clearly.*

Wednesday a retired missionary spoke to the prayer meeting at the Baptist church. He talked about church people doing more in world missions, especially overseas. Virginia listened with joy. She knew she had her sense of direction. After the meeting, she talked with the missionary briefly, confiding that God was speaking to her about foreign missionary service.

On the way home she felt sure about the foreign part. She was comfortable with the idea of teaching.

But India?

Later that night, packing to leave for home the next morning, she stopped to browse a bit in the book her high school group had given her that day. The first article concerned a Muslim prince—a young Indian, supremely confident in his religion.

Virginia couldn't explain why, but she had part of her answer for a second time. She could see herself teaching young people like that Indian prince.

All summer India continued in her thoughts. The idea of unknown difficulties to be encountered in a foreign country proved strong encouragement in the hard spots of her summer work in the Columbus Baptist Association, not far from her home.

When she talked with her parents about what she was feeling, they made her very happy. "We would not like to see you go so far away," they told her. But, they assured her, she must know that they would never stand in the way of God's leading.

The India part was still a problem. She wrote a friend, expressing concern that Southern Baptists had no missionary work in India. Her letter brought a quick reply and a news clipping about a Southern Baptist missionary, expelled from China, who had just visited India in the hope that Southern Baptists could work there.

She read a book on missionary preparation and that fall—1949, the second year in Reidsville—she wrote to the Foreign Mission Board of the Southern Baptist Convention.

By now she was reading everything she could find about what Southern Baptist missionaries were doing overseas, and where. Country by country her scrapbook grew, with particular attention to work among Muslim people.

When the Reidsville people began to learn that Virginia would not return another year, that she was planning to resign to attend seminary, they asked her to reconsider. They were insistent, but she could not stay. She had discovered what the Lord wanted her to prepare for.

Seminary Experience

"Okay, Ginny. Stash the books."

With senior-class-to-junior authority, Virginia's roommate her first year in seminary explained that open house was one of *the* events on the campus social calendar.

At least the women's dormitory residents at Southwestern Baptist Theological Seminary took their open house seriously. They made great preparations to invite the student body and faculty in to inspect their premises and enjoy their refreshments. At the last minute it was Virginia's idea that if they left the closet door open, their room would look larger.

"Extra depth, extra space," she insisted.

By the end of open house the two of them had gained rather much attention, not for the spaciousness of their quarters but for the fact that they alone, of all the dorm occupants, had opened their closet for inspection.

Always in the daily schedule, study was Virginia's highest priority. She chose heavy content courses. Old Testament. New Testament. Ethics. She added a part-time job in one of the administrative offices, and weekend work in a local Mexican mission. Trying to get to know the youngsters she taught on Sundays, Virginia experienced firsthand all the ghetto problems there are. Poverty. Overcrowding and malnutrition. Strained relationships. Inadequate materials to work with. Church discipline.

During the first year, also, came the news that the possibility of Southern Baptist work in India was out, at least for the present. Maybe the Lord used my interest in India as a way to get my attention, she decided.

"So what now?" her roommate asked.

"I believe I'm willing to go anywhere the Lord leads, or to stay at home. But I feel a definite interest in Muslim people."

As much as other studies allowed, Virginia kept gathering information about Christian work among Muslims.

When school was out, Virginia went to California for a summer's work under the Home Mission Board. Upon returning, she found seminary life even busier than before. Early in the school year the missions committee—Virginia was on its planning group—began working on the Week of Prayer for Foreign Missions, an annual observance scheduled for early December and always climaxed by the Lottie Moon Christmas Offering for foreign missions.

"Everybody went all out last year," she reminded the committee. "Let's work for a deeper spirit of sacrifice this time," Virginia suggested.

After a few circle meetings around the dorm, a Week of Prayer schedule was set, and with it, an offering goal of $2020 for the seminary, with this slogan: "20/20 Mission Vision."

"Remember," the new students pleaded, "we are poor and struggling. Everybody is!"

The goal stood. By Halloween many in the dorm had already begun to take on extra jobs. Some sold blood. Some skipped meals. The student body as a whole entered into the effort to have a significant part in the Week of Prayer. Everybody was encouraged by the fact that the year before 175 girls in the dorm had given more than $2,000 to the total seminary offering. There was a particular thrill in being a part of an undertaking of the whole Southern Baptist Convention.

During this missions emphasis, Virginia Cobb submitted her final application papers to the Foreign Mission Board. Prayerfully, she applied to work in Jordan.

"The group that has challenged me most, and has seemed most neglected through history and now, is the Muslims," she wrote. "My lifework purpose is to do all in my power to extend the kingdom of God. As a teacher I should expect both to win people to Christ and to help them to grow into mature Christians and workers."

She told her parents that although Baptist work in Jordan was comparatively new, she had met a couple headed there for medical work, and had learned that the missionaries in Jordan had plans for a school.

"So I am anxious to go," she told them, "and shall if I pass all those examinations."

As her application was processed, the FMB personnel department authorized physical and psychiatric examinations. Then in March, Virginia, and 24 others were invited to attend the April 1952, meeting of the Foreign Mission Board.

"Wonderful feeling!" she wrote home. "Nothing more to hinder between me and the mission field (although the psychiatrist did push me about how I think I will handle the problem of loneliness overseas, being single as I am). Appointment is what all this study and work has been for. It is rather humbling to see the task and one's own inadequacy, but the certainty of his calling and the assurance of his grace are enough.

"I've been corresponding with a girl in language school in Beirut. Her description of the needs makes me all the more anxious to go. The Muslim world is so huge and so hard of heart and so neglected. It is one of our newer fields but seems to me quite strategic. Surely we're not just prejudiced in thinking that foreign missions is the very cutting edge of God's kingdom."

Missionary Appointment

Sunday travel was unusual for Virginia Cobb, but the first Sunday in April 1952 was different. Between four in the morning in Fort Worth and midnight in Richmond, Virginia, she moved closer to the formal beginning of her missionary service overseas. The seven-minute flight to Dallas, the plane changes there and in Washington, put her and Charlene Jones, another missionary candidate, in Richmond in time for a quick supper, the evening service at First Baptist Church, and a late get-together with the other appointees.

Monday was a blur of touring the Foreign Mission

Board building, attending staff prayer meeting there, being photographed and introduced many times; all this before lunch. The afternoon was filled with practical matters. Available discounts for cameras. Summer school plans. Sailing information. In the evening there was an orientation dinner.

"We're not appointed yet," she told her mother and father on the phone. "Tomorrow morning we go before appointment committees—individually. They must vote us in."

In the committee interview, Virginia answered questions about her background and Christian experience.

"At age eight I felt I should join the church and after talking with my parents and our pastor, did so in all sincerity. Later, in high school, I wasn't so sure. I listened more carefully in church and studied the Bible diligently because I wanted to know how one really was saved.

"In my concern I prayed, 'Lord, I don't know how to be saved, but you do; you'll have to do it for me.' "

"You found the satisfaction you were looking for?" a committee member asked.

"Yes. I did, and I learned what it means to trust."

"And about missions?" another committee member inquired.

Virginia recounted her plans for a chemistry major in college and her hopes to do research. She recalled a Sunday night sermon which sent her home wondering why she wasn't comfortable with the idea of a research job with opportunities to witness and spare time to use for God.

"I knew God wanted all my time," she continued.

"And I promised it to him.

"For a long time I wasn't sure what, but a missionary's prayer meeting talk at the end of my first year teaching school brought the almost surprising conviction that God did want me as a foreign missionary, primarily to Muslim people."

The committee was satisfied and that night—a Tuesday in April 1952—it was. After reports by the Board's president and the executive secretary, Dr. M. Theron Rankin, each of the 25 missionary candidates made a brief statement. After that, there was the official vote for appointment. Dr. Rankin spoke to the group and presented a certificate of appointment to each appointee.

Wednesday morning the Board meeting continued. That evening Virginia and several other new missionaries who were taking a late flight to Washington were invited to visit in one of the Richmond churches.

Night flying was exciting. Virginia especially enjoyed the view of the nation's Capitol and the Washington Monument floodlighted against the sky. With her friend, Charlene Jones, she had to change planes in Washington. Charlene's ticket was for a 1:25 A.M. flight; Virginia's for a flight ten minutes earlier. They were told there was no chance to travel on the same flight, but while they sat in the crowded terminal waiting to leave, an airlines representative came looking for them with word that there was space for Virginia on the 1:25 flight.

"Imagine that! Those people sought me out in all that crowd. And with a refund too." Virginia was elated. And after the nonstop flight to Dallas and an hour's wait there, she and the others were back in Fort Worth, having missed only the first hour's class. Seminary friends welcomed them back warmly. One even presented Virginia with typed notes for the theology classes she had missed. A graduate student gave her a small mimeograph machine for use in her new work.

Virginia found herself really looking forward to Beirut ("such a modern city, I don't need to stock up on a five-year supply of toothpaste and the like; it's a place where you can buy furniture, china, stove, refrigerator—whatever"). Summer school kept her in Fort Worth until almost time to leave, and naturally, there was much talk about missions and missionaries. One professor always greeted her as a "real live missionary!"

"But I feel so humbled," Virginia confessed. "So far I'm that in name only and doing no more than anyone else would if called to do it. None of us have proved ourselves yet.

"By the way," she added in a letter home, "I'm not sure whether I will work in Lebanon or Jordan, but it matters very little to me. For two years I will be in Beirut learning the Arabic language, and then it will depend on the needs and the opportunities."

PART TWO

PREPARING—ON THE SPOT

There is no way to exaggerate the potential strength of a ministry which combines evangelical theology with fearless mentality and a genuine concern for people.

ELTON TRUEBLOOD

Fall, they say, is Lebanon's least beautiful season. The humidity is at its worst. Summer's heat has seared the once-green earth, and the winter rains have not yet come. But, mid-September, 1952, arriving for the first time, Virginia Cobb was thrilled with its beauty. No matter where she looked, the mountains above Beirut seemed to be picture-book country. Despite a few modern touches, the small villages beyond the city reminded her of Bible stories.

Beirut itself captivated Virginia. She never tired watching the people in this Mediterranean city. And as she learned to recognize them in terms of their national origins, the more she felt the weight, and the potential of the opportunity before her and her fellow missionaries in the city, not to mention the rest of Lebanon and the whole Arab world.

Martyr's Square, she soon discovered, was a place to study people, Lebanese history, and the missionary task. The monument from which the square took its name, she learned, was a memorial to those who died in the war for independence before the founding of the republic. The people who frequented this square—a busy bus terminal area—provided Virginia a kaleidoscopic view of the Arab Middle East.

There she saw Kurdish women, distinctive in their

full-length brocade skirts and flowing white head-dress. Most Kurds, she was told, still lived in the borders of Turkey, Iran, Iraq, and the Soviet Union, but a substantial minority, persecuted in Iraq, had come to Lebanon. It was known that most Kurds maintain contact with their relatives in other countries. *What if a Kurdish woman were won to faith in Jesus Christ,* Virginia wondered, *and told other Kurds about her experience?*

The Armenians Virginia saw waiting across the square probably were Lebanese citizens, but their forbears came from around the Black Sea and some of them were refugees. These people also maintained contacts with their own relatives throughout the Near East.

Watching people come and go, Virginia decided that the black-robed priest—the one with the knot of hair on his neck, looking like somebody out of Leviticus—must have been Greek Orthodox. She knew that his people were descended from the earliest Christians in the area of Lebanon; that the Orthodox, the largest Christian group in the Middle East, maintained connections with many of their number living in Greece and Russia, as well as in the countries immediately surrounding Lebanon.

She soon learned to spot a Druze, perhaps by his beard but certainly by his short jacket and pointed shoes. She also learned that his people, respecting ties of family and clan, came to be known as an offshoot of Shi'i Islam, a group whose practices include some elements of Christianity, whose homeland is southern Syria and the mountains of Lebanon.

Before going to Lebanon, Virginia had read much

about what she would find there. The variety of the people. The fanaticism and fear of change. The surfeit of powerless religions. The group consciousness which makes it hard to leave one's traditional religion. The persecution and ostracism which result when a person decides to leave his place in society for the sake of a small, locally "unproved" movement.

The New Testament makes reference to Paul's visit to Phoenicia (an ancient country located where Lebanon is now) on his way to Jerusalem, and to the fact that he found brethren there (Acts 21:7). But Christianity in what is now Lebanon, as in much of the Middle East, lost its vitality. Only after the middle of the nineteenth century did missionaries from the West begin work in the country.

The American University in Beirut, now nonsectarian, was founded by Presbyterian missionaries in 1866. Soon thereafter, in 1883, a Lebanese photographer, Said Jureidini, was converted and baptized into a Baptist church while on a visit to the United States. He returned home zealous for his newfound faith. Occasionally, after 1922 a missionary in Palestine, Dr. J. Wash Watts, visited Lebanon. By 1927, Southern Baptists were giving some financial aid to Mr. Jureidini's work, and since 1948, Southern Baptist missionaries have lived in Beirut.

The first ones, Finlay and Julia Graham, who had been in Nazareth and Taibeh prior to the establishment of the state of Israel, found 22 Baptists in Beirut, members of two small congregations. The Grahams were soon joined by two young women and a medical couple. By the time Virginia Cobb arrived in 1952, there were only three in Lebanon, the medical couple having gone to Jordan and one of the young women having resigned.

Lebanon Beginnings

The first day she was in Lebanon, September 17, 1952, Virginia Cobb learned the Arabic alphabet. Her teacher was the young son of the Grahams. Everybody noticed her eagerness to begin, but who could have foreseen that this quiet girl, slow southern drawl and all, would come to be recognized as the best Arabist in the Baptist mission?

Soon after her arrival, Virginia began studying Arabic with Salim Freiha, a believer, a Presbyterian of Greek Orthodox background, who had accepted responsibilities as language teacher for the Baptist Mission mid-January 1951.

The language study pattern was individual study and daily tutorial sessions with Mr. Freiha. A basic curriculum was evolved in the mission, with specific blocks of material to be covered in given time periods.

Virginia consistently took four hours of tutoring a day, from the first. And along with this, she used at least six hours a day in private study. Patient and cheerful with his students, Mr. Freiha encouraged Virginia, as he did all the missionaries who studied with him. The first indication of things to come was noticed when Virginia finished the basic two-year curriculum in eleven months.

Soon after getting settled in Beirut, Virginia talked with the leaders of the Beirut Baptist Church (as it was called then) about her desire to become a member of the congregation.

They agreed, and from the outset, she was impressed by the congregation. The required waiting period before new converts were accepted for baptism and full membership was something Virginia had not known in the United States, but she observed that those who were members of the congregation were faithful, and well-grounded in the Scriptures.

Even though she understood very little of what was said in the beginning, Virginia identified herself with congregational activities. She attended the Bible studies at the church two nights a week, and in the afternoons, study groups for women and girls.

"They all pay close attention," she noticed. "They take part in the discussions and really dig deep into the meaning."

Virginia saw the same pattern of Bible studies at two preaching points away from Beirut. She decided that these Lebanese Christians would continue to grow spiritually as long as they stayed close to the Bible.

Soon after her arrival, Virginia was invited to go with some of the church women to a preaching point an hour's drive from the city. At the stone house to which they had been invited, they found ten village women. One of them, older and dressed in the typical black dress with scarf, wore no shoes. Two or three of the younger ones appeared much less provincial.

The Bible study centered on the first chapter of John. At the outset the village women were quiet, leaving most of the discussion to their visitors from Beirut. It was obvious that some of them could not read, but the "meeting together for study" was a significant beginning.

The village study was also another evidence of the

growing maturity of the Beirut church. As she got to know the members individually, Virginia was impressed by their strength and testimony. Not a large congregation, as people often think of churches in the United States (only eighty baptized members), but a courageous one. Most of the members were tithers, despite meager incomes. Most of them were regular in attendance at the congregational meetings, and willing—eager—to witness to other people about their faith.

Virginia noticed that some of the young men arrived for the evening Bible studies almost breathless. She learned that they had come directly from the day's work without taking time for supper. She soon saw that problems affecting any member's testimony were considered serious congregational concerns— with discipline so severe that the average easygoing American church member would soon find himself excluded from the fellowship.

In the Sunday School, Virginia noticed that there was no literature—except for a Bible story her missionary colleague, Mabel Summers, translated week by week.

She and Mabel, apartment mates for a long time, often discussed Christian opportunities in Lebanon. As they would staple the Arabic Bible stories to the English-language lesson leaflets they used (because people liked the pictures on them), the two talked about the young people in Lebanon and their hopes to reach them with the gospel.

The few young people who were in the Baptist congregation encouraged Mabel and Virginia. They knew that the gospel could be meaningful to countless hundreds of Lebanese youth if only they could discover ways to reach them. At the same time, it was necessary to face the fact that many obstacles faced the young people in the church who were eager to spend their lives in the Lord's service.

For one thing, there was the matter of education. Without public education in Lebanon, many were unable to afford schooling. The Baptist mission and other groups helped a few who showed promise for the future. But even after high school, the problem persisted because of the scarcity of Christian colleges or seminaries.

Yet one has to be among the Lebanese only a short while to realize that if a person aspires to preach or teach, education is a must. The Lebanese share with all Arabic-speaking people a deep feeling about their language and its proper use. Classical Arabic, quite different from the everyday speech of homes and marketplaces, is still used in public speaking. Bad grammar, or unclassical expressions, reflect upon the person who speaks poorly, and are considered an insult to the language.

The consciousness of this feeling was enough to keep Virginia at the study of Arabic. But there were other considerations, too. The more she learned about the people, the more she recognized the place of religion in their lives and the dimensions of the missionary task in the Middle East. Studying the various religious groupings around her, Virginia discovered how complicated the relationships between the groups were.

The strongest Catholic group in Lebanon, the Maronites, constitute a national church loyal to the

Pope in Rome. But there are also Greek Catholics and Greek Orthodox Catholics in the country. By virtue of the slight majority of Catholics in the Christian population, the laws of Lebanon prescribe that the president must be a Maronite. The law also provides that the prime minister must be a Muslim.

Because of its Muslim population, Lebanon is joined to the Arab world, an allegiance which exists among the diverse peoples who use the same language—Arabic, the language of the Koran—and follow a life-style that has evolved from the teachings of the Koran's sacred text. All over the world there are said to be almost 500 million Muslims. Of these, 100 million are Arabs. They live in Syria, in Iraq, all down through Arabia, and across vast stretches of north Africa. They live in Jordan, in the Gaza Strip and, of course, in Lebanon.

Most students of religion agree that Muslims hold to their faith with a fanaticism and zeal unequaled by any other people on earth. They also agree that the Christian religion meets its strongest opposition among Muslim Arabs.

Virginia knew about this resistance to Christianity before she went to the Middle East. She had studied enough to understand some of the basic reasons. But it all came alive in Beirut.

There the small congregations of Baptists, despite their depth of Christian fellowship, were in fact a minority sect largely confined to their own quarter of the city. Lebanese they were, yes; but evangelical Christians in the Arab world, in a Muslim culture.

After three months in Beirut, Virginia wrote home that "work among Muslims requires patience, and a willingness to wait and work slowly with few visible results."

First Look Ahead

The first Christmas in Lebanon, 1952, Virginia's thoughts turned to her family in Georgia. There was joy knowing of their interest in what she was doing. There was the exchange of gifts across the miles, and much mail.

Her mother, involved in the observance of the Week of Prayer for Foreign Missions in Statesboro, wanted help "straight from the field," as she told the women at the church.

"Ginny," she wrote to Beirut, "send me something I can use at the church."

What she received was more than all the Baptists in Statesboro could easily respond to in terms of the prayer and giving required to set forward the gospel witness in Lebanon.

"Since Lebanon is a country of religious freedom and is fairly up-to-date in some ways, and accessible, it seems the logical center for work throughout the Muslim world.

"At present the only other Baptist work in the Arab Near East is in Ajloun, Jordan, where we have a new hospital with three doctors and their wives appointed to serve there.

"May I let you in on the dreams we have for the future?

"We foresee a day when the Southern Baptist Convention will become greatly concerned for the millions of Muslim Arabs, and send out many missionaries throughout all this vast area. There will be centers—strong centers—everywhere to witness to the Light of life.

"In the one place where Muslim intolerance does not deprive people of all religious freedom—right here in Beirut—we shall have a printing press sending out literature for all Arab-speaking people, to help with Sunday Schools and chapels and Bible teaching. There will also be a school here, going all the way through college and seminary, to train Arab Christians going out into the Muslim world, and so that Baptist children will not have to attend expensive Catholic schools.

"Is this too much to ask for?"

Without even giving the reader time to reply, Virginia went on to outline details for the school she and her colleagues hoped to bring into reality. Then she reminded her mother, and others, about other needs.

"The small beginning work now in Tripoli might blossom into a center for the whole northern part of Lebanon, if an evangelical missionary couple could be placed there. Sidon is the logical place for another evangelistic couple to guide the mission in Mia Mia and to work in the south of Lebanon."

In an added word to her family, Virginia told them she felt she was beginning to make some progress in Arabic.

"I'm unable to render any service now," she continued, "except for study itself, but I do hope it won't be too long before I'll be able to do better."

Fellow Christians

Study remained Virginia's number one priority all

through the first months in Beirut. But after a year she was reading from the Bible, and the Koran, in Arabic. In a way, study remained the priority of all the years she spent in the Middle East. Fortunately for her, however, and for the Baptist witness in the Arab world, she was able to finish the formal language study period without major interruption. In fact, ahead of schedule.

The same month she passed the formal language study milestone, April 1954, Virginia moved to Ajloun, Jordan, to meet an emergency situation in the Baptist school there. A month later she was also serving as secretary of the Arab Baptist General Mission, the organization of Southern Baptist missionaries in Jordan, Lebanon and Gaza.*

The move to Jordan was for one year, for by the end of language school Virginia Cobb requested assignment to Lebanon—for literature work.

When the school year closed in Jordan, Virginia moved back to Beirut, ready to involve herself in the work to which she was to give the rest of her life. Never a prolific correspondent, she advised the Foreign Mission Board of her new publications responsibility by a brief change-of-address to *The Commission*: "Please change my address from Baptist Hospital, Ajloun, H.K. of Jordan to Near East Baptist Mission, Box 2026, Beirut, Lebanon." And except for two furloughs in the United States, here she spent her life.

The year Virginia taught in Jordan, missionary

---

* In 1954 Southern Baptists entered Gaza to take over a hospital operated for a hundred years by the Church Missionary Society (CMS) of England.

colleagues in Beirut began a nursery class in preparation for the formal opening of a school. In October 1955, the dream of a Baptist school in Beirut became a reality, with 99 pupils enrolled in two kindergarten classes and grades one through four. No matter that it would be eight more years before the first high school class would be graduated; or that the building was still incomplete. The Baptists were on their way in education.

School chapel services were planned for the auditorium of Beirut Baptist Church. By the Mission's deliberate decision, the church building and the school building were located adjacent to each other.

When all the construction was finally completed, the Baptists rejoiced because their facilities attracted attention in the city. People came in off the street to ask about the Baptists.

"All the people are talking about this new building," a neighbor told one member of the congregation. 'People are asking who the Baptists are and what they teach. They say they want to know more about the Baptists."

The missionaries realized that the buildings in themselves were important in Beirut. The church, with the school beside it, demonstrated to the community that the Baptists were not just a small sect that would appear and then vanish. Both buildings were received as evidence of the Baptists' determination to stay, to be a vital part of the community and of Lebanese life.

The day the church building was dedicated, Virginia thought she had never seen such interest in the Baptists. The President of Lebanon attended, and so did the American ambassador. The missionaries had also expected the Lebanese prime minister and his cabinet, but that very morning their government fell from power and, understandably, they were involved in other activities.

Pastor Elias Saleeby introduced a member of the congregation, Mrs. Salim Sharouk, an evangelist's wife, who presented a Bible to President Camille Chamon.

"Mr. President," she said, "this Bible is a gift from the women of Beirut Baptist Church to you for Mrs. Chamon."

A representative of the Foreign Mission Board, Dr. George W. Sadler, then area secretary for Europe, Africa, and the Middle East, spoke to the people who overflowed the 600-seat auditorium for the dedication service. Because many visitors who were not Christians were present, Dr. Sadler spoke directly to them.

"The members of this church have had a peculiar spiritual experience with the Lord Jesus Christ which is called the new birth," he explained. "And it is this experience which has made them join together to work and to worship and to serve."

Virginia's response to the new building and its meaning for the gospel was sheer joy. Sitting in the service, she whispered to herself a verse from Matthew, Jesus' words: *What I tell you in darkness, that speak ye in the light: and what we hear in the ear, that preach ye upon the housetops* (Matt. 10:27). In her mind the gospel *whispered,* as it were, in the hearts of the congregation was now indeed being told in public. Hardly anybody noticed the "Baptist church" sign long over a doorway leading upstairs to the former meeting room of the congregation. But here she was in a building that attracted attention. And here were many people—officials, reporters, the curious—gathered from many parts of Beirut.

People can see us now, she kept saying to herself. *People now know that there is a Baptist group in their midst.*

Virginia prayed that the congregation's testimony, and with it her own, would always match their visibility in the community.

Sunday School classes now had places to meet, both in the church building and in the school. Virginia thought she had never seen the boys and girls in the Sunday School so wide-eyed as the first time they met in the new building.

"The assembly period," she said, smiling, "went off with unaccustomed reverence."

Weekdays the building's rooms were used for church meetings, the school chapel services, and for many special meetings. Some of the space was used by missionary language students. And, especially important for Virginia Cobb, was the workroom set aside for publication work.

Education and Literature

With its new building, Beirut Baptist Church faced broadened opportunities to teach the gospel. The work in both Tripoli and Sidon was growing, and there were several other chapels as well. The Baptists in Lebanon began feeling the need for a coordinated program of education. In 1955, Virginia Cobb was asked to try to coordinate Sunday School work for the churches, and to promote better methods.

Among the missionaries there was concern for

Sunday School work geared to all ages; for Bible teaching to win converts, to nurture young Christians, to develop congregations deeply concerned for those around them.

Virginia saw her job as threefold: (1) to develop a complete, graded set of Sunday School literature with teachers' helps; (2) to develop a complete set of teachers' and pupils' materials for Bible study in Baptist day schools; (3) and to survey all available Christian literature in Arabic to see what "can be used and what must be produced by us."

She was sure now that literature provided one of the best ways to reach the Muslim world. She kept thinking about the junior high school girls near Ajloun. The first day a shelf of Arabic literature was available to them in their school's modest library, they checked out half of the shelf's sixty volumes.

Already she had learned that though much literature was available in Arabic—everything from Shakespeare to Grimm's fairy tales to agricultural methodology—all the Christian books in Arabic taken together would fill only a small shelf.

"Christians," Virginia told her colleagues, "cannot afford to delay in the task of exploiting the powerful medium of the printed page to set forth the claims of Christ in every area of life."

Her reasoning was based on a sense of priority about the gospel, as well as on a growing awareness of Arab feelings about literature and language.

Visit any mosque. Walk in the public buildings of Beirut or, better yet, a city like Cairo. Spend time in a museum anywhere in the Arab world. Or just look around in the brass shops of the market places.

THE GIFT OF BELONGING

What do you see? A motto. A proverb. A line of poetry. Always in beautiful Arabic script.

His language and literature is dear to the Arab, Virginia learned, because its importance is related to his faith and tradition. In the Islamic view of life, the preservation of God's Word has always been primary. In fact, Islamic tradition insists that, according to Muhammad, the most severe punishment is reserved for those who portray God's creation. For this reason painting, sculpture, and music have suffered severe artistic limitations in Muslim societies. Not so with calligraphy and literature. Among Muslims, literature—especially poetry—is considered art, as is the actual writing of classical Arabic. And always the devout Muslim carries the word of the Koran in his heart.

School children memorize texts from the Koran. When the Koran is used in mosque services, it is quoted in Arabic, or read from beautifully written copies.

A favorite pastime, especially among Bedouin Arabs, is a literary contest in which each one must quote a line of poetry beginning with the last letter of the line he just heard. Even illiterate Muslims commit to memory lengthy portions of the Koran. Of poetry too. And Arab people, in general, seem to gain a particular thrill from hearing an eloquent passage of Arabic.

Virginia Cobb thought she saw another reason for developing Christian literature in Arabic.

She had already heard, and soon discovered for herself, that it was extremely hard to witness to Muslims in public. Few would enter a church. In fact, not many willingly engage in conversation with a Christian, be he Arab or missionary. Few Muslims want to risk being seen accepting Christian instruction. But, reasoned Virginia, a book or a tract. . . .

Silent witness that it is, the printed word can reach the hand of a person who would never dare enter a church building. The book or tract can be where the Muslim is, ready for its message to be taken to heart at any time—many times over—by many people at the same time.

Looking back, Virginia Cobb saw those mimeographed Arabic Bible stories she and Mabel Summers stapled into English-language lesson leaflets for what they were: first steps on the road to usable, attractive Bible study materials in Arabic.

April 1954, they had their first Sunday School quarterly. Mimeographed. With pictures pasted in. By the next winter a printed quarterly, and a series of simplified lesson leaflets for the younger children were ready. Plus teacher's helps on two instructional levels. By the spring quarter 1956, with increasing acceptance, a weekly circulation of 1,000 was reached for both quarterlies and lesson leaflets. Pictures still had to be put in by hand. But modest age-graded Sunday School materials were in use in Lebanon, Egypt, Jordan, and Gaza. And Virginia was involved in the preparation of graded Sunday School literature to be used in rotation within department age-levels.

By this time also, women's and girls' groups in several of the churches in Lebanon needed something to supplement their Bible studies. Occasionally a member of one of the girls' groups, one who knew English, translated and presented a missionary program. Women's groups which included a missionary in their membership also received current missionary information. To help out at this point, Mabel Summers led in preparation of a set of twelve missionary programs soon made available to all Arabic-speaking Baptists.

Such programs, in the hands of young women in several of the churches, later involved them and Virginia and other missionaries in a social ministry in the Karantina section of Beirut.

With Sunday School and missionary materials underway, the next step was the preparation of a small book on the meaning of church membership. This was accomplished by the work of a national pastor who re-edited a book used earlier. Another major effort was to begin preparation of teacher's guides and pupil's workbooks for Bible study in all grades of the Baptist day schools in Lebanon, Jordan, and Gaza. Virginia's goal was to see at least two grades in every school using these materials in daily Bible studies by the fall of 1956.

As she studied the materials of other Christian groups in the Muslim world, Miss Cobb was concerned to avoid unnecessary duplication of effort and product. After evaluating her own beginnings in publication, she felt the efforts made were typically Baptist; that is, concerned with Bible teaching materials for the on-coming generation.

"Our beginnings are extremely small," she said. "But we know One who multiplied a boy's lunch to feed thousands, and by his grace our small efforts may be magnified and made more effective."

Beirut Base

Beirut, the location of this publication work, was not an important city in biblical times. However, it had played a significant role in the Middle East. And in the 1950s, as Southern Baptist missionaries continued to become better acquainted with the city and her people, their feelings deepened about its strategic importance for any Christian witness among Muslims.

Obviously Beirut was, and is, a transportation hub. One of the main international airports for all the Arab Middle East is there. The city serves as a seaport for Jordan and Syria, and to some extent for Iran and Iraq. Businessmen of the Arab world congregate in Beirut, and many others seeking business in the Arab countries establish headquarters in Beirut. Many financiers are in the city. Also, many international business offices are located there, as well as the prestigious American University which was originally a mission school.

Important for Christian missionaries is the real-if-fragile balance of power existing between the Christians, mostly Catholic, and the Muslims of Lebanon.

For Southern Baptists, other missionaries continued to arrive to add their strength to the work begun. The David Kings came to help with theological education; the J. W. Trimbles and the James Kirkendalls for church development responsibilities, and others. Sometimes singly; usually couple by couple.

Always before the Lebanon Mission—the organization of Southern Baptist missionaries in the country—was work to be done and the necessity to determine priorities.

Just after Beirut Baptist Church dedicated its new building, the four Baptist congregations in the country held revival meetings.

"From the beginning we sensed something different about these meetings," Virginia recalled.

Participating in the advance planning and prayer support, the evangelistic effort brought to Beirut Baptist Church, Virginia felt a new sense of purpose.

"We organized ourselves into 'Encouragers' to encourage the people who raised their hands in the services and remained afterwards for counseling, and 'Guides' to talk with the seekers about salvation and Jesus Christ.

"The new building was a great advantage. People could sit comfortably and hear clearly.

"The first night ten or twelve people stayed after the service to talk with some of the 'Guides,' and it was the same every night. Among those who responded were family members the congregation had been praying for so long. Some were students in the new Baptist school. Some, young people reached through the Sunday School. And some, our neighbors and acquaintances who had seen the difference Christ makes in a person's life."

"How does one join your group?" one young Muslim asked.

Being told about the times of the church services and invited to attend, he persisted: "No; I mean, how can one join and be a part of your group?"

The young man listened carefully to Virginia's explanation of Christian faith. He accepted a New Testament. He explained that he was seeking for himself the same life-style he had seen in a Christian man he knew.

Another young Muslim moved into the neighborhood of the Baptist church and, curious about what went on in their building, attended a service. He found himself interested and began to attend weekly Bible study. After a number of months, and patient counsel by the church's evangelist, he determined to become a Christian.

"When he gave his testimony to the congregation at a Wednesday evening meeting," Virginia said, "we all cried."

This young man, a college graduate, spoke quietly and clearly about his experience. In conclusion, he shared the praise and thanksgiving of his heart to God in a poem he wrote for the occasion:

"You are my pride, my glory, O Jesus!"

"If you know Arabic poetry," Virginia said, recalling the young man's confession of faith, "you know how moving it is; how it moves the hearers. That's why we cried."

Being moved to tears by Arabic poetry was a sign of Virginia's growing involvement in Lebanese life, or more specifically perhaps, with Arab culture.

The language fascinated her. Challenged her. Got her up early in the morning for study, a habit that, once begun, marked all her years in Lebanon.

"Virginia just plain loved Arabic," Mabel Summers said, in retrospect. "A good memory is important to learning Arabic and she had that. She had good pronunciation, and natural ability for the study of language."

The more Virginia steeped herself in Arabic, the

more committed she was to putting the Christian message into the language and getting it out to the people. The more involved she became in the work of the churches, the more she longed for ways to break out of the narrow confines of congregational life, isolated from the mainstream of Arab life. The more she worked with fellow missionaries, the more she felt the urgency of the mission task in all of the Middle East, a task she increasingly defined in Arab and Muslim terms rather than just Lebanese terms.

Nevertheless, Beirut was her city. And more, she came to think of it as a base of operations for activities which she earnestly prayed would reach out to Muslims wherever they were.

For all these reasons, Virginia Cobb rejoiced when the Southern Baptist missionaries in Lebanon, Jordan, and Gaza organized themselves into the Arab Baptist General Mission "to better carry out our work as one mission and to point out the one factor that binds our three countries together."

The missionaries in these three places continued to work at the local level in their respective countries. In Arabic. For the salvation of Arabic-speaking people. But beyond that, together they sought ways to communicate the gospel in Arabic.

As Virginia soon learned, the Mission—any Mission—is a way of life. A full-time responsibility basically without a job description. A team effort involving, paradoxically, a degree of freedom few other life-styles afford. And simultaneously, a servant role disciplined by private and group experiences with God.

Every time the Arab Baptist General Mission came

together there was some pressing, puzzling matter affecting the Christian witness they were all trying to make.

In 1954 it was the question of who should be admitted to the Baptist schools.

One missionary felt that those who seemed unlikely to become Christian believers should not be admitted.

"The educated Muslim probably would not help our testimony."

"How about a compromise?" Virginia countered.

Her idea was that if all children were admitted to the elementary schools, regardless of their family's religion, but that admission to the high schools be on the basis of having attended a Baptist elementary school, the opportunity for witness to each one would begin sooner and last longer.

Another missionary preferred no distinctions, period.

It was finally decided to leave the matter to the Mission's education committee.

At that time Virginia was not on the education committee, but she was on the language committee and the literature committee. And she was on a committee to name and define the functions of all Mission committees.

From the time of the organization of the Arab Baptist Mission in 1954, there was a growing sense of wholeness in the missionaries' approach to Christian witness in the Middle East. As a group they looked forward to the time when "the work," as they put it, could be turned over to Christian nationals.

Inaguration of the first major mission institution in Lebanon, the Beirut Baptist School, was considered a step in this direction. Likewise, the literature production was aimed at serving the Baptists in Arabic-speaking churches.

October 1956, the Lebanese Baptist Convention was organized.

The next spring Virginia Cobb reported to the Arab Baptist Mission that Bible study materials were ready for the day schools, grades one through five; that the available Vacation Bible School materials were appreciated and were being used; and that the continuing preparation of Sunday School materials was on schedule.

In midsummer 1957, Virginia left Lebanon for her first furlough to the United States.

"The full term of service for me has fallen roughly into three sections," she wrote the Foreign Mission Board. "First, a year and a half in language study in Beirut; second, about a year and a half as principal of the Baptist School in Ajloun, Jordan; and finally, two years engaged primarily in literature production in Beirut."

During the furlough, she studied again at Southwestern Baptist Theological Seminary, completing two semesters of graduate work with a *straight A* average. When school closed in May, Virginia went home to Statesboro to prepare for her return to Lebanon. But news from the Middle East was ominous throughout the spring and summer of 1958.

Early in the year, Gamal Abdel Nasser had led Egypt and Syria to form the United Arab Republic which declared itself dedicated to uniting all the Arab nations. Lebanon, the next-door neighbor to Syria, soon found itself gripped by terrorism and appealed to the United Nations. Just months before, President Eisenhower had sent the U.S. Sixth Fleet to the eastern Mediterranean to discourage Syria's designs on Jordan.

Mid-June the travel agent advised Virginia that her visa had not been granted and that if it was not received by the last week in the month, her flight, set for July 2, would have to be delayed.

Late June, no visa. The second of July a cable went from the Foreign Mission Board to the Jordan Mission: "Could you accommodate Virginia Cobb for indefinite period?" Five days later an affirmative reply was received. But in the meantime the visa was granted, and on July 10, Virginia returned to Beirut.

Four days later King Faisal of Iraq was killed and his government, considered pro-Western, overthrown in a revolt thought to have been Nasser-inspired. By this time Lebanon was engulfed in civil strife, and mid-July President Chamoun appealed to the United States for help, and President Eisenhower ordered U.S. Marines from the Sixth Fleet into Lebanon.

In quick sequence, Premier Khrushchev called an emergency meeting to deal with Middle East problems, and President Eisenhower suggested a meeting within the United Nations Security Council. Russia, at first, accepted this proposal, then turned it down. All the while the unrest inside Lebanon continued, with complex political and religious overtones. In five months of fighting several thousand people died.

In Beirut the severest fighting took place in the Musaitbeh community where the Baptist church, school, and missionary apartment building were—and still are—located. Many people left the city, and for a time most of the missionaries moved out to safer parts of Beirut.

By December some semblance of normalcy was restored. Both Lebanese Christians and missionaries, reflecting on what had happened, decided they now had a second chance to bear their witness.

Due to furloughs of school personnel, Virginia was pressed into service at Beirut Baptist School this first year after her own furlough, in addition to her literature work.

Over the New Year holiday she attended a Sunday School curriculum workshop in Beirut to plan materials for youth and young children; and also to review basic aims and principles in Sunday School work.

"The gospel," Virginia insisted to her colleagues, "has never yet made the impact on the Muslim world that the risen Christ is most certainly able to make.

"Is God," she asked, "waiting for us to take up that burden more seriously in prayer and faith?"

Now into her second term in Lebanon, Virginia Cobb was strongly convinced that literature was strategic for Christian witness in the Muslim world. As a result, her commitment to this approach and her work load grew.

The literature committee of the Arab Baptist General Mission, in correspondence with the Sunday School Board of the Southern Baptist Convention, received permission to reproduce any pictures under the Sunday School Board copyright. Also, an editorial procedure was worked out whereby manuscripts in Arabic would be checked at least three times to insure the best possible translation with particular attention to the quality of English-to-Arabic idioms used.

In its 1958 meeting, the Mission elected Virginia secretary and also named her to two committees: literature and language. Within the year, the literature committee was renamed the "publications committee," and in 1959 the Mission acted decisively to give its publications committee responsibility for the literature to be used by the Mission as a whole, and authority to organize itself in such a way as to see projects through to completion.

Also, the publications committee itself had one recommendation: that Virginia Cobb be named coordinating director for Baptist publications. She had been in Lebanon seven years. A full decade of work in Arabic language publication work lay ahead.

PART THREE

DOING—AND LEARNING

The vocation of the Christian is threefold: He is called to *pray,* to *serve,* and to *think,* and he is called to do all three together. . . . The best thing we can do for our troubled world is to increase the number who, because they are committed to the threefold pattern, are the genuinely new men of our time.

ELTON TRUEBLOOD

In the early months of 1960, Baptist Publications moved from the cramped workroom in the church building to a location on Mar Elias Street, a few blocks from Beirut Baptist School.

Two apartments there, owned by the Lebanon Mission, provided first-floor space for literature storage, as well as a publications office.

That summer Virginia Cobb reported to the Arab Baptist Mission that Baptist Publications was expanding both in volume of work and facilities.

"We are in the process of equipping these quarters for the committee's work, though the equipment is minimal.

"The Publications Committee takes seriously its obligation to all the other committees and agencies of the Mission," she reported, "to provide printed materials for their use."

Also, Virginia reminded her fellow missionaries of the committee's continuing responsibility to survey the field of Christian literature for the Arabic-speaking world in order to fill content gaps and to cut down overlapping.

In this work Virginia Cobb hit her stride. She did some translation work herself, and much editing of translation done by other people. She handled administrative details of printing and distribution, as well as planning with and for the Publications Committee of the Arab Baptist General Mission, and surveying of Christian and other literature available in Arabic.

In the midst of all this, Virginia continued to be active on the local scene—in the Lebanon Mission, and among her fellow Christians, especially in the Baptist congregations she knew best.

At the same time, she enjoyed life tremendously. She developed a life-style geared to her work. Living alone at times; but more often with a fellow missionary, Virginia found relaxation in flowers and birds, and her tawny red cat, Spoofy—and the kittens. Sometimes there were occasions out, like dinner at a favorite Austrian restaurant.

Books belonged too. Theology and history and Islamics. Mathematics; through calculus yet. Music. Greek-English and German-English lexicons; plus Hebrew. Many books in English; but more in Arabic.

Routinely, her days began early. There were quiet times with devotional classics, and always the Bible and prayer. All this before the five-thirty-in-the-morning Arabic classes. After the basic studies in Arabic were finished, Virginia moved ever deeper into the language and literature, with attention to Islamic classics and to studies in content areas where Christian materials were badly needed.

Publications Office

In Beirut's cool seasons, when the publications office was cold in the mornings, Virginia used small propane heaters. Having lit the stove in her secretary's office, she would adjust her own and then get to work, her feet curled under her in a blue wool shawl.

"Good morning, Marcelle!" Virginia always heard the key in the door and recognized her secretary's step.

"Good morning to you!"

Before long the two of them would be going over the day's schedule.

"Miss Cobb, do you know that boy, Hasan—he visits here sometimes? Yesterday he wanted to borrow one of our books." After a moment, Marcelle added her question: "What would you think?"

"About his borrowing a book?"

"Yes, for an English assignment." Marcelle still remembered her own high school days. She knew how hard it was for many students to find the reading material they needed.

With page proofs due the printer before noon, there wasn't much time to talk about how the publications office could lend books. But it was an idea. A good idea.

Especially was it a good idea when you think about the people who come in. Young people needing this or that typed for use with a church group. Others just wanting to talk. The publications office had a reputation for friendliness. All the Baptists, in fact, knew that the people in that office were always thinking about the churches and the kinds of literature the members could use.

Marcelle had first met Virginia Cobb at church. Because of her mother's faithfulness to the church, Marcelle Nasrallah could not remember when she had not known Miss Cobb.

Often this young woman thought how interesting it was to work at the publications office weekdays, and then to be in a church where the published materials were used. She wondered if the members of the Sunday School in her church, or any of the other congregations, really knew how much work went into Christian literature. Hours and hours of translating, writing, proofreading, checking orders.

Often, returning from lunch, she would see Virginia still at her desk.

"Miss Cobb, did you have any lunch?"

"Yes, Marcelle," she answered, smiling. "Candies and coffee."

Meeting at Emmaus

Always looking for ways to get Christian literature into the hands of more people, Virginia stayed with her missionary assignment. A close observer of life around her, she kept asking questions. *What are the Baptist church members doing to make new friends? Do they witness to their neighbors? to the people they contact in the course of a day's work? What can evangelical Christians do to share their faith beyond the church buildings? What points of contact do we have with Muslims here in Lebanon? in other Arab countries? Is there one question Muslims especially want to ask about Christianity? What about the Baptists, especially the adults, who have few opportunities for study? Is there something we can suggest beyond the Sunday School lessons?*

Virginia came to the conclusion that there was more that could be done. Midsummer 1961, she proposed to the Arab Baptist Mission that the Bible study materials being prepared for the six secondary school grades also be used for study course materials.

"We have two Baptist high schools," she reminded her colleagues. "One in Beirut and the other in Ajloun, Jordan. Why can't we make the Bible study materials used in the schools available to a wider circle of people?"

"Are there other books already in Arabic which could be used in such a study program?" one member of the Mission asked.

"What about some system for people to earn some recognition for particular studies?"

After discussion, it was agreed to refer the recognition possibility to the Mission's Religious Education Committee, and to ask Virginia Cobb to furnish that committee a list of books and other materials suitable for a study course plan.

As is always true in Mission meetings, the annual get-together is a time for reports, business sessions, worship, vacation, fellowship, and strategy planning all rolled into one. Whenever the Arab Baptist General Mission held a meeting, it was an event of at least several days—usually a week or more. Between business sessions and times set aside for worship and study, mission meeting was—is—a time for members to catch up on one anothers' happenings, a time to share joys, disappointments, recipes, and remedies for children's illnesses; a time to encourage each other, to be renewed both in spirit and group unity for the common task.

Emmaus, midsummer 1961, was such an occasion; one in which it was hard not to be aware of where they were—in a Jordanian town with a long history, one intimately connected with Jesus' earthly life. An awesome experience in a way, but not so as to preclude the consideration of mundane and practical matters related to their team effort in Jesus' name.

"One little matter," Virginia said during one of the miscellaneous business sessions. "It's about requests from churches to the publications office for typing and mimeographing and—well, you all. . . ."

Everybody smiled. Virginia thought she heard sighs of sympathy from several places in the room. Everybody present understood the need to deal with small expenditures as well as major budget items.

"I mean . . . paper and ink cost . . . well, somebody has to buy what we use. Plus time that staff people have to take from their work. We want to help, but. . . ."

"Why don't you charge for services rendered?" The question came from the back of the room.

"We may have to," Virginia admitted.

"I move this Mission grant Baptist Publications authority to set prices and make charges for extra mimeographing."

The motion, made by one missionary, was seconded by another, and carried handily. So, too, did the recommendation that T. B. Maston's book, *Right or Wrong?* be translated into Arabic and then published.

Committee by committee, groups in the Mission with specific assignments and responsibilities, made reports, sought counsel, talked about plans, and presented recommendations.

Looking to the future, the publications committee noted that Sunday School and Vacation Bible School materials for a three-year cycle would be completed "in the next two years," and that certain publications needed to be continued; for example, organizational program materials, theological textbooks, tracts for Muslims, a book on how-to-do-it for Sunday School methods, biographies in Arabic, and books on how to teach the Bible to children.

In one brainstorming session somebody wondered aloud if study course books translated into Arabic for use in the churches could not also be used for a correspondence course.

A long discussion ended when Missionary Jean Dickman, a physician from Gaza, moved a recess for picture-taking—and coffee.

Before the Emmaus meeting ended, the matter of programming for radio and television came up for discussion. The Mission chairman asked Bill Hern and Virginia Cobb to inquire about the availability of free time for broadcasting from Lebanon and Jordan "as soon as Arabic materials are ready."

No one mission meeting ever provided all the answers. Major discussions, as at Emmaus, move into the background pending concensus, but are seldom forgotten.

After Emmaus, Virginia Cobb, for her part, was continuing the search for meaningful Christian-Muslim encounter.

Here they were—these missionaries—living in a country where the Koran was revered and quoted among Muslims much as the Bible among Christians. With mosques and daily prayer calls almost more visible in the city than church buildings and Christian witness, Virginia was struggling with the problem of meaningful contacts with Muslim people. She knew a few Muslims; all the missionaries did. But what could she say, or do, to get beyond the speaking acquaintance stage with the people she wanted most of all to reach for the sake of the gospel?

Should Baptist Publications be devoting so much of its time and energies to materials for church organizations? she wondered. *Wasn't there any effective way to reach out beyond the Christian community? Was Islam really as impenetrable as people seemed to think?*

Karantina

The questions did not go away. Neither did the work at hand. For Virginia, one part of that work was meeting with young women's groups in two of the Baptist churches in Beirut. For a long time she had been active with this age group in Beirut Church, the congregation meeting in the building next door to the school. Later, her major effort was put in the newer Ras Beirut Baptist Church (and after the organization of Ras Beirut, the first Baptist church in the city was usually referred to as Musaitbeh, a designation of its location in the Musaitbeh area of the city).

During a city missions emphasis in 1961, Virginia suggested to the young women in the two churches that they take a close look at their city. They did. Some of the members went around taking pictures in various sections of the city. Its landmarks. Its scenic places. Some of the residential areas. And also pictures of Beirut slums, including Karantina, the "slum of the slums."

"We showed the pictures at a joint meeting of the two groups," Virginia said, "and presented a challenge: here is our city; what are we going to do?"

"Those slum pictures; where did they come from?" one girl asked. "I've lived in Beirut all my life. I just didn't know there was such a place in our city."

"Miss Cobb, are you sure?"

The questions were serious. The girls were sobered by what they saw. Makeshift housing. Ragged children. Open sewers. Muddy paths where you would expect streets. Refuse everywhere.

"Let me tell you about a woman who lives in Karantina," Virginia responded.

She told them about the Kurdish woman who cleaned apartments in many houses around the publications office. She recounted how she and Marcelle, seeing the woman in the neighborhood, began to talk with her and learned who she was. Desperately poor, and far from her family, this woman lived in a tin shack in Karantina.

"I've been to see her a number of times," Virginia told the girls.

"I think we ought to go to this—this Karantina," one of the girls blurted out, "and share what we can."

"We don't have much money for food or to buy clothes," another reminded the group.

"I mean we should share Jesus," her friend rejoined.

"But we can't go there," a third one insisted. "Karantina is Muslim."

However, the girls did go. With Miss Cobb and others giving what assistance they could, two rooms were rented in a tin-can shack. The girls themselves went through the neighborhood inviting children in off of the streets. Since the Karantina was "strictly Muslim," they decided it would be best to begin slowly.

"Let's just start off by saying that God is love," they agreed.

From the beginning there was interest. A hundred kids crowded into the tiny rooms. There were no chairs. Probably nobody missed them, and for sure nobody minded sitting on mats on the floor.

"There were so many that *we* had to stand outside," Virginia said.

Order was a problem. That is, for those who thought Sunday School should be a quiet time where people just sit and listen. Not those Karantina kids. They came and went as they pleased. They talked aloud. They interrupted the teacher. And sometimes, if the idea caught their fancy, they threw something. Dirt clumps. Food scraps. Sometimes a rock. Little by little the idea of giving attention to what was going on was introduced. Singing together caught on. In time the Karantina kids learned to enjoy coming together whenever those girls from the outside opened their small rooms for songs and Bible stories.

The girls, along with two Beirut Baptist School teachers (both Christians but both formerly of the Druze sect of Islam) and the missionaries who worked with them—Virginia, Mabel Summers, and others— soon discovered that they could say whatever they pleased.

"Nobody gave a hoot," Virginia reported.

The girls told the Karantina kids that Jesus was God's Son. Everybody thought that was great. The girls told the story of Jesus and the Samaritan woman. Word got around the Karantina that those Baptists were talking about the way people live, and how best to do it. More youngsters kept coming. And a sprinkling of older ones as well.

Finally, they found a larger meeting place. The new room was up a flight of stairs, but no matter; that just provided extra seating space for those who still couldn't get inside. The next big step was taken when it was decided to divide those who came into groups.

"Twenty in a group in one room," one suggested would be ideal. Things never did work out ideally, but the Sunday School kept on and weekday group meetings were added. A woman's group was especially well attended.

Still, those who worked in Karantina learned that they had to use some kind of an "on guard" procedure. The whole area was so conditioned to anger and brutality that sometimes, even in a Bible study period, violence would flare. If one child thought another one got the pencil he should have had, a fight was sure to follow. The same thing might happen if the pieces of candy didn't get distributed exactly even, or if one child blocked another's view of the teacher.

Some of her colleagues still remember Virginia's telling them about "that Khalif" who had decided he did not want to be one in the group on a particular day. One of the Baptist girls was teaching Khalif's group a new song. Virginia was "on guard." Somehow Khalif slipped away from the group. The first thing anybody noticed was an old chicken foot thrown into the room through a small hole in the window. By the time Virginia missed Khalif, and then located him on the stairs the next floor up, another piece of rotten food and a stone had sailed in through the open window.

When Khalif was discovered, naturally he ran. So did Virginia—chasing him down the street to explain that he didn't have to come but that if he did. . . .

Reporting back to the Musaitbeh congregation, Virginia explained that it was sometimes difficult to work with the people in Karantina "because they are undisciplined. They like to smear mud on a car and will, once in a while, throw garbage.

"But generally," Virginia insisted, "these people love those who come to them. They respond. They are teachable.

"Many of them—well, those that are Palestinians, are provided for by UNRWA. The Lebanese among them can go to a government school. But the Kurds and the Syrians, these people have less opportunity. And lots of kids there, girls especially, just don't go to school."

The Karantina project continued. It served the dual purpose of focusing some Baptist attention on one of the troubled spots of their city. It provided a point of contact with people who were not Christians.

Karantina, the Baptists learned, was actually a squatter area. The people there put their tin shacks on somebody else's land, and there they stayed. Since the early 1950s there has been talk around Beirut about clearing the slum area to make room for cheap public housing. But still new people are constantly moving in—mostly Kurdish people who are Palestinians from the south of Lebanon, largely Shi'ite Muslims.*

---

* Shi'ite Muslims are a minority sect in Islam who consider that the descendants of Ali, Muhammad's cousin and son-in-law, are

"The people in Karantina can only think of getting," Virginia explained.

"If you took scraps of cloth in there for a sewing class, say, some of the girls would spend half their time hiding the cloth under their skirts. But then we came so far with one group that they made a quilt—well, actually they knitted an afghan and sent it to refugees in Jordan.

"When they got a letter back from the people who received their gift, they wanted to do more. You see, some of them had learned to think of other people; a big, big accomplishment."

Hartford

In early March 1963, Dr. Cornell Goerner, then FMB secretary for Africa, Europe, and the Near East, received a letter from Virginia Cobb in Lebanon.

"Perhaps it is not too early to write you about my furlough plans," she began.

There was some detail about dates in the letter. Virginia wanted to stay in Lebanon through the Baptist World Youth Congress, set for July that year. Then this:

> I had for sometime considered going back to Southwestern to finish the B.D. degree I have been working on since 1952. However, as I have prayed about the matter, it has seemed that some study of Islam at Hartford Seminary in Connecticut would be far more beneficial to our total efforts here. Some of us have a growing concern that so little of our work is directly aimed at the Muslim people, who are the majority of the Arabic-speaking people. Even in our publica-

the prophet's legal successors; they reject all other caliphs and the Sunnite orthodox legal and political institutions.

tions work we have almost nothing specifically prepared for them and almost no one qualified to do so. Therefore, whether or not I can complete this degree there, the study there seems to be the most important thing and is, as far as I can tell, the Lord's leading to me.

"With Dr. Goerner's encouragement (Hartford has the strongest program in Islamics in the United States) we ought to have some people who are aiming directly at work among Muslims." Virginia used the time, midsummer 1963 to midsummer 1964, for furlough. Furlough from Baptist publications and Karantina and the Arab Baptist General Mission. But no furlough from her ever-deepening desire—no, determination—to penetrate the Muslim scene, at least in Lebanon and, hopefully, beyond.

After the youth congress in Beirut, the travel to the United States, and a visit with her family in Statesboro, Georgia, Virginia went north to Hartford.

When the matriculation formalities were finished, she was a candidate for the M.A. degree in Islamics. This means, she wrote, "that most of my work can be of direct help in understanding the Muslims."

One unexpected opportunity at Hartford was being asked to help with the teaching of beginning Arabic. The young Egyptian who was to have come for this assignment, ran into passport complications which made it impossible for him to travel.

At Hartford, Virginia's fellow students included missionaries from a number of Christian groups who shared her compassionate concern to reach Muslims with the Christian gospel. The teaching faculty, she found both knowledgeable and stimulating.

While there she began a study of the mystic, al-Ghazzali (1058-1111), a Muslim scholar whose work and example in the practice of mysticism, as opposed to knowledge about it, built lasting bridges between contending Islamic factions. In al-Ghazzali, Virginia came to grips with the scholar's discovery of contradictions in his religion; that is, the paradox and problem of the Koran with its strict judgment and Islamic tradition with stress on great mercy and almost unlimited forgiveness.

To fulfill the degree requirements, Virginia undertook a thesis which included a study of al-Ghazzali's theological thought and a translation from Arabic to English of his *Dhikr Al-mawt wa ma ba'Duh,* "The Thought of Death and What Followed It," the concluding book in al-Ghazzali's forty-volume work, "The Revival of Religious Sciences."

It was Virginia's feeling that the discussion of "last things" must inevitably imply a certain view of history and of man. Likewise, she felt that the fact of death always posed questions about the meaning of life, and that the mention of judgment must include the meaning of sin and the way of salvation. Therefore, she concluded that an eschatological study must necessarily touch on a number of important ideas, and thus provide fresh insights about Muslim thought patterns.

Her translation, over 400 pages in English typescript, with an introduction about al-Ghazzali's place in Islamic theological thought, was accepted by Hartford. The thesis was actually completed after Virginia's return to Lebanon, so the M.A. degree was granted *in absentia.*

Damascus

Soon after Virginia Cobb began her third term of missionary service overseas—in the fall, 1964—the publications committee of the Arab Baptist General Mission held a long meeting in Damascus. They met for a week, in fact. It was a "think-tank" experience familiar to every missionary involved in determining the "tactics" to be used in a particular situation to implement mission strategy. Call it evaluation. Call it discussion. Call it hard work. By whatever term used, it was a group experience of prayer, consultation, proposals, and counterproposals; a time to face problems, to clarify objectives, and to share with one's colleagues in the gospel.

Virginia was there. So, too, were Bill and Vivian Trimble, Lebanon missionaries, particularly concerned with the distribution of literature; the couple who had filled in for Virginia during her furlough. Violet Popp was there. A nurse stationed in Jordan, Violet was a member of the publications committee, its secretary. Jim Powell was there from Lebanon; Anne Nicholas and Ava Nell McWhorter from Gaza. Also Alta Lee Lovegren and Frances Fuller from Jordan.

Everybody had done some homework. Between them the committee members laid out before each other: (1) a materials distribution report; (2) a publications market study; (3) a study of Baptist materials with attention to gaps in subject matter; and (4) a companion study of types of Christian literature being produced by others working in the Arab world.

"One of the most difficult hurdles in the way of

progress for Baptist Publications is the matter of getting published materials into the hands of readers."
Virginia thought this meeting was a good opportunity to try to see the whole picture at one time. So she continued, "And then, of course, there's the matter of getting the materials read. If we fail here, we must admit defeat in the aim and goal of publishing.

"Books left to catch dust on the shelf don't help anyone. Obviously all publishers—large or small, religious or secular—face this problem. Witness tremendous advertising campaigns and the free spending of many publishers to promote their books."

"Is the Arab world a special case?" the missionaries asked themselves. Everybody knew that the evangelical community was extremely small in the total population. Nobody knew better than they that non-Christians are hesitant to be seen purchasing a Christian book, or even inside a religious bookstore.

Another fact of Baptist publications concerned the necessity to provide materials openly promoting the Baptist cause. Who else except Baptists need literature with a Baptist slant? And what about costs?

Every missionary in the meeting could name congregations having difficulty buying even the minimum materials needed for Sunday School classes. Everyone present had had the experience of hesitating to recommend a certain book to a person in one of the churches because it cost too much.

"It's pretty hard to decide to buy a book when the alternative is less food on the family table," Bill Trimble said.

The committee members talked about the limited number of teachers and leaders in the churches.

"Better trained leaders will encourage the use of literature," Frances Fuller suggested.

Everybody agreed this was true. And thinking of the congregations each knew best, they all realized that training leadership was a long-range proposition. This consideration then brought up the fact that certain books have been published because they are badly needed, in spite of the fact that there will always be a limited number of people needing them. Seminary textbooks, for example.

"Another thing," Jim Powell offered, "how many religious bookstores are there in Lebanon? Or how many secular bookstores in the Arab world carry any Christian books at all?

"Plus the matter of border regulations," Violet Popp added. It was common knowledge that government regulations often slowed down the shipment of materials from one Arabic-speaking country to another.

"Not to mention the problem of getting money out of some countries to pay for books." Bill Trimble was well acquainted with this problem because of his work in literature distribution from Baptist Publications in Beirut.

When the discussion turned to distribution, there were several matters the Trimbles could report. They were sure that Baptist Publications materials were being sold in six bookstores: two in Jordan, two in Lebanon, one in Tunis, and one in Switzerland. And in Beirut they had contacted bookstores-other-than-Baptist as well as some of the small street book stalls with encouraging initial results. They did notice an interest in books and in reading on the part of seminary students. They did feel that such interest would

forecast well for the future when these men themselves became pastors of congregations with responsibilities for leadership training.

The Trimbles reported "book days" in some of
the Baptist schools and the possibility of subsidy to
churches for the purpose of buying literature.

"Too, we hope the recent actions to reduce prices
will prove a definite statement in the direction of
making books and materials available."

Since everyone had been present when the Arab
Baptist Mission approved price adjustments for Baptist Publications, it wasn't necessary to spend much
time in that discussion. Everybody joined Bill in
hoping that lower retail prices would mean higher
distribution figures for Christian literature produced
by Baptist Publications.

The committee brainstormed ways to acquaint the
public in general, and Baptists in particular, with
available materials. They decided that they must
make contact with every religious bookstore serving
a sizable Arabic-speaking population, and send them
catalogs. Also, they must contact book sellers. And
they must investigate the possibility of some book
consignment plan whereby dealers could pay for
materials as they are sold.

What about book stalls on the streets that we would
operate ourselves?

What about portable bookstores to travel to small
villages?

What about publishing some books with a more
popular appeal, and yet with a basic Christian message?

What about a series of newspaper articles within

the framework of existing budgets?

The "what abouts" grew to be so many that everybody realized it would be necessary to determine priorities, to set a few directions and pursue them, rather than to keep too many projects active at the same time.

The committee formulated and adopted a statement of operating principles for Baptist Publications, laid plans for a workshop for Arabic-speaking writers to be held in August 1965, and projected a correspondence course project "to reach as many people as possible who might not otherwise attend local Baptist churches."

Before the meeting adjourned, Jim Powell pointed out the need for published materials especially for Muslims, and Virginia Cobb talked about the need for a book on Islam especially for Christians.

"What we really need," she explained, "are two books—one on Christianity for Muslims and one on Islam for Christians—to help improve communications between the two peoples, to encourage true acceptance by each group of the other, and to interpret each group to the other."

The committee agreed that these materials should be produced in consultation with Muslim leaders. They also agreed to begin with a pamphlet for evangelical Christians to be followed by four books on these subjects: (1) Islam, a book especially for Christians, (2) Christianity, a book especially for Muslims, (3) thoughts about Christ, a compilation of statements by outstanding non-Christians, and (4) a book on the living Christ today.

Everybody recognized that it might take some time

to work out details for such a series of books, but the committee was unanimous in its evaluation of their importance.

In other actions, the publications committee voted to begin the translation of Jesse Fletcher's *Bill Wallace of China* and to undertake an anthology of present-day Christian martyrs. And also to suggest that the music committee study the possibility of producing a Baptist hymnal to meet various church needs.

Before adjournment, the Committee agreed to seek wider distribution for everything prepared by Baptist Publications, to do a better job of publicizing Christian literature, to sponsor a writers' workshop, and to publish new materials including "several books aimed to promote understanding and friendship between Muslims and Christians."

There was one other decision: to study the possibility of moving Baptist Publications to new quarters in a Muslim area of Beirut.

Reporting to her own Mission in Lebanon, Virginia Cobb asked for prayer in the implementation of the decisions.

In her own private times of prayer and meditation, Virginia acknowledged the heavy work load and her own dependence upon God's grace. With joy and determination she committed her best to her job. With her colleagues, Virginia was optimistic in the face of too much to do. And, to their dismay, she was addicted to thinking up more jobs, or so it seemed.

One more evidence of her wholehearted commitment to the gospel and to evangelization came to light when the minutes of the fall meetings of 1964 were mailed out to the Lebanon Mission. Sandwiched between reports from the evangelism committee and the visual aids committee was a five-page paper entitled "Projected Plans for the Future." The paper was unsigned, but marginal notes on the first two pages were in Virginia Cobb's handwriting.

"Please note," the paper ended, "this is the work of one person dreaming out loud. No action has been taken by anybody, nor is it anything more than a suggestion of some possibilities."

Everyone in the Mission read Virginia's dreamings-aloud appreciatively because they all knew her ability for keen analysis.

What Virginia did not realize at the time was how much a new missionary, a young schoolteacher who had arrived in Lebanon a few days after her return from furlough and Hartford, would soon become involved in her dream's fulfillment in unexpected ways.

"O wow, Virginia," this newcomer, Nancie Wingo, said to her the next time they met, "don't you ever do anything but work?"

Beirut

Work was always the order of the day at Baptist Publications. But for all that met the eye, much of the labor was done behind the scenes. Often with the assistance of missionaries not officially related to publications.

With the help of Frances Fuller and Jim Powell, a series of newspaper ads took shape. Three Beirut newspapers began running the ads in January 1966. In the first ads, the copy was a brief discussion of some topical subject from the Christian perspective.

As response increased, the column grew into a weekly question-and-answer feature. Also early in the year, this modest notice was run in the papers:

> Free correspondence course on the life of Christ; Scripture included. Will be mailed to you in a plain, unmarked envelope.

Both the newspaper ads and the correspondence course were carefully planned. And audacious. All the records in hand at the time indicated that the outreach of Baptist Publications' materials was pretty local. But from the beginning, Virginia Cobb and others associated with Baptist publications in the Middle East thought of their work as a multicountry ministry.

True, the first aim was to produce curriculum and other materials needed by Baptist churches and institutions. But even so, some of these, particularly Vacation Bible School literature and Bible study materials prepared for schools, proved attractive to other evangelical groups as far away as the Sudan.

As the scope of productions gradually broadened, a few materials of interest to all Christians were published. A student's Bible atlas, for instance. Then the translation of a few novels and children's books with a Christian message.

These materials proved marketable and by the time the newspaper ads were instituted and the correspondence courses ready, Baptist Publications was dealing with Arabic-speaking groups in Israel, Syria, Switzerland, Morocco, Tunis, and Egypt. There were also occasional contacts with church groups in Aden and Tanzania, a few mail orders from Iraq and Kuwait; even a few inquiries from Arabic-speaking groups in South America.

The first series of newspaper articles brought five hundred letters from eight countries, including Nigeria. As advertising was stepped up, response to the correspondence course increased as much as 200 a month.

"In addition to their lessons," Virginia reported, "our correspondents sent us questions—personal, spiritual, intellectual; and sometimes their pictures and life stories, or pictures of their countries.

"More than a hundred of the correspondents have asked to be introduced to someone nearby to help them with the lessons or other spiritual matters. We have been able to put a number of them in contact with nearby pastors or believers known to us. But more than half of them are out-of-reach, except by mail."

The mail response raised new hopes for witness.

The Mission continued to be concerned to use every means possible to reach Muslims with the gospel.

"If we really want to develop a broader ministry," Virginia insisted to the publications committee—and to everybody else who would listen—"it depends on two things. We must produce more books with a broader appeal and we must advertise and contact bookstores in many countries."

As the aggressive ministry of Baptist Publications kept growing, it became more and more evident that the modest offices on Mar Elias Street were too small. There was only one small counter to handle book sales. Hamid Hoshi, a newcomer to the staff, was willing to help every customer who came in, but there was no place to put new materials.

Marcelle Nasrallah was hard-pressed to find room for the contact files, or to arrange desk space for those helping with the correspondence work. Atiah Hadad found it almost impossible to handle the necessary shipping and mailing of curriculum materials for churches and schools. With stock piled everywhere, it was obvious to everyone who came around that the publication work had outgrown its facilities.

Virginia Cobb was sure that now the time had come to implement the Damascus decision to relocate. The question was where.

"Marcelle," she began as they talked together one morning, "what would you think about our moving to the Basta, to Abu Haydar Street?"

It was a cold day and not too many people had been in. Virginia had just made a cup of coffee and was about to settle down to finish a galley proof due within the week. For a few moments Marcelle did not answer. Then one word, a question:

"Why?"

Before Virginia could reply, Marcelle went on.

"Miss Cobb, already I am worried because you and Miss Nancie Wingo are living in that neighborhood. And now you want me to go to work there every day? What will my mother think?"

"She is a believer, too, Marcelle."

Marcelle nodded. This was not a new subject for her to discuss with Miss Cobb—the relationship of Lebanese Christians to their Muslim compatriots. She knew well the fears of church members, and the long record of Christian-Muslim misunderstandings.

"Marcelle, I am tired of staying so long on the

border."

After a pause, Virginia continued: "I want to go inside to reach the people. Even if we aren't able to preach freely, we can show them Christ."

"Miss Cobb, what will the people in that neighborhood think?"

"Look at it this way, Marcelle. We are people. They are people. We speak Arabic. They speak Arabic. Every day, going about our business, we can speak to people. They will get to know us."

Marcelle nodded.

"Then, Marcelle, what if, in addition to our work, we can have some contact with people in the neighborhood? Maybe a bookstore. Or—well, maybe a reading room where people would feel free to come to read; maybe even to talk."

All through the fall of 1966, Virginia Cobb and others related to Baptist Publications continued to look for a place to move. Even those against the idea of a Baptist office in a Muslim neighborhood agreed that the time had come to move. Somewhere.

Most buildings in Beirut that could possibly be considered were of one type construction: garages on the ground floor, or small shops which were really just one room. Virginia knew that if they were to have a bookstore, they would have to find some ground-floor property. And in her own thinking, she was willing to settle for a ground-floor room with an apartment upstairs, despite the inconvenience of having to run up and down stairs from office to bookstore. In her own mind, Virginia was committed to a Muslim community. Like the Basta.

In that exact community the committee found a

new building with *two* ground-floor apartments opening on the sidewalk level; a building only a block or two from the Saudi Center and adjoining mosque. The king of Saudi Arabia had provided funds for both the mosque and the community hall; thus the name, Saudi Center.

Could they possibly secure that ground-floor space? The committee's investigation revealed that one of the ground-floor apartments was already rented, but one was available, and also the apartment above it. Thinking that such a find would be the best they could possibly do, the publications committee agreed to negotiate with the owners to buy the two apartments they had been shown.

The owners seemed willing enough to talk with the Baptists, but soon reported that they had bad news.

"We had to sell the upstairs apartment," the property spokesman said. "Could you be satisfied with the two ground-floor apartments?"

"Malish, never mind," Virginia said, trying to contain her joy, "we'll take the ground-floor space."

Before long the word was out to all the Baptist churches in Beirut, and also to many persons in the Basta: Baptist Publications is moving to Abu Haydar Street.

Local Baptists were quick to point out how dangerous it would be for the employees. Also, how inconvenient it would be for everybody who had to go there for materials needed in the churches. The staff was less than enthusiastic, but at the same time, each one felt a sense of "oughtness" about their work.

Virginia herself was prepared for many questions.

They came. She remained undismayed by hostile statements. They came, too. Not unexpectedly. Patiently she talked to all who asked about the move. Undoubtedly there would be long months of getting-acquainted. Yes, she expected there would be misunderstandings to overcome before the Beirut Christians, who were known as Baptists, and the Muslims in the Basta would accept each other.

"Nevertheless, the committee responsible for the decision to move to Abu Haydar Street," Virginia said many times, "felt it was following clear leadership from the Lord to make this venture in understanding, despite much objection by the Lebanese Baptists."

البحر الأبيض المتوسط

ايـــران

العراق

مصر
م.ع.ع

شبه
جزيرة
العرب
السعودية

السـودان

جمهورية الكنغو
وسط افريقيا

At the Baptist Center, Beirut, Lebanon, Virginia Cobb points to a map which indicates the outreach of Baptist publications. Her life was dedicated to spreading the gospel in the Arabic language. (FMB photo by Fon Scofield)

نرجو المعزرة

لقد افتكرنا بانكم تقوموا باعمال
سياسية ضد العرب ولكن كما ظهر
لنا من الكتب والرسائل الموجودة
لديكم لا تتدخلوب في السياسة
بل فقط في القضايا الدينية . لذا
نرجوا ان تسامحونا

اخوانكم

A note left by those who looted the apartment of Virginia Cobb—the text: We beg your pardon. We thought you were engaged in political work against the Arab, but we noticed from books and letters that are present that you are engaged in religious matters and not in political matters. Therefore, we beg that you will forgive us.

(signed) *Ikhwatukum*, your brethren (FMB photo)

Here Miss Cobb and Chassen Khalaf discuss a question received from an enrollee in the Bible correspondence course. Khalaf served as lesson grader for the course. (FMB photo by Fon Scofield)

Miss Cobb's work was highly diversified. Although the Director of Publications, she did not remain tied to an office. She was constantly among the people. Here she is with a group of youngsters in a Bible study meeting. (FMB photo by Paul S.C. Smith)

The scene is the Baptist Publications Office in Beirut. Virginia Cobb and her secretary, Marcelle Nasrallah, enjoy a good, hearty laugh. (FMB photo by Al J. Stuart)

Miss Cobb and Hamid Hoshi, Book Store Manager,
stand in front of the Baptist Center in Beirut. There
is superb teamwork in carrying the printed message
through books and periodicals. (FMB photo by Fon
Scofield)

Regardless of the language, errors are possible. Here Virginia Cobb reads a galley proof printed in Arabic. (FMB photo by Fon Scofield)

At the Baptist Center, Hamid Hoshi, Book Store Manager, and a young man carry on a conversation. The locale is the reading room where many questions are answered. (FMB photo by Fon Scofield)

No wonder Virginia is smiling! This display represents the wide variety of books published by her office, books that have carried the message of Christ throughout Lebanon and surrounding countries. (FMB photo by Al J. Stuart)

In this shot Virginia simply poses and looks straight at the camera. She is surrounded by Sunday School literature for Arab readers. (FMB photo by Al J. Stuart)

Virginia Cobb welcomes a young man to the bookstore at the Baptist Center. The public is encouraged to come in and browse. (FMB photo by Fon Scofield)

In the Publications Office, Director Virginia Cobb leafs through a display of literature. She had a strong sense of mission and satisfaction as the gospel of Christ was sent throughout the Arab world. (FMB photo by Fon Scofield)

PART FOUR

BEING PRESENT

. . . Paul shared the secular life of people before he spoke to them about religious matters. To this concept modern Christians and others are returning. Mission is seen to be the activity of a man who does a useful piece of work in the world (other than proclaim religious truths) but chooses to do so in a sphere where he is exposing himself to an alien culture and familiarizing himself with it.

W. MONTGOMERY WATT

Even before all the preparations to move Baptist Publications, Virginia Cobb and her missionary colleague, Nancie Wingo, were making a personal venture in understanding among the Arabic-speaking Muslims in Lebanon, the country to which God had led them.

Nancie was still in language school and both of them were living not far from Beirut Baptist School, close to others in the Lebanon Mission. Virginia, with her own teaching background, kept in touch with the school. Some years she carried school responsibilities; always she could be counted on in emergencies. The two of them worked in local Baptist churches and in the weekday program in the Karantina.

Unable to get away from her strong desire to live in a Muslim neighborhood, Virginia asked Nancie if she would be interested.

Of course she was. In fact, before missionary appointment, it had never occurred to Nancie that she would live anywhere else than in the midst of people who were not Christians. Somehow she had missed the fact that there were cities where living quarters followed religious lines.

Looking around for suitable places, they found two

apartments in exactly the neighborhood they wanted—in the Basta—about six blocks from the school,
and about three from the new publications office.
When all the arrangements were completed, they
became across-the-hall neighbors on the fourth floor
of a new building. Their landlady, who lived in the
same building, became a good friend. And in the
time they lived there—more than a year—Nancie and
Virginia got acquainted with all the people in the
building.

Besides that, they had grand projects. Like a visit
to every family in the building once a month. That
particular project wasn't always realized as fully as
they would have liked, but they did find many occasions to invite groups into their apartments. Also,
they enjoyed getting acquainted with the shopkeepers
along their street. Being the only Americans in the
neighborhood, Virginia and Nancie were something
of a curiosity at first. But as they visited around, they
discovered that their landlady had already introduced
them. Proudly.

Living in the Neighborhood

"Hey, Nancie; pull that chicken out of the oven
and come on."

This particular evening, Virginia had met her
weekday class in the Karantina, checked by the publications office and made it home before Nancie got
in from language school.

By now the two of them had decided it was more
fun to eat meals together—when they were at home,
that is. They both looked forward to supper time,
a quiet interlude in the day. Until they got the hang

of it though, there were numerous trips from one apartment to the other, depending on where they were eating, and who was fixing what.

Virginia had the table set. And the salad was on. She had even remembered to pick up a couple of pastries; (un)fortunately for them, there was a bakery not far down the street. She had the record player going; Jascha Heifetz, a favorite concerto. Her cat, Spoofy, had been fed. Also, the geraniums watered and a check had been made on the balcony garden. No snapdragons yet. But a few nasturtiums, some unwanted Johnson grass and an unidentified little white thing.

"Sorry. Running late today," Nancie explained, forking golden brown chicken onto each plate. "I've got rice. You've got greens. Guess we're eating healthy, huh?"

"And wait till you see what's for dessert."

"Praise the Lord. How scrumptious! *L'Hamdillah.* Amen."

"That's how you get so much done, Nancie." Virginia was already spooning rice onto her plate. "You're direct. You skip fancy words where action's called for."

Lingering over a third cup of coffee, the two continued talking.

"All the feast day preparations on the street look big," Virginia said. "Palm branches. Lights. Goodies. Real exciting—except that it reminds me how far we are behind on visiting the neighbors."

"Okay, Virginia. You forget editing. Forget correspondence. I'll forget grading papers. And that horrible class plan past due. Let's visit everybody in this building—tomorrow."

Some of the neighbors Nancie and Virginia had not really met. They could recognize most of them though, just from their goings and comings in and out of the building.

Next day, after lunch, two floors up from their apartment, they stood at the door of one of the families they had often greeted in passing. Sometimes in the elevator.

"You ring," Virginia said.

"No, you ring."

When courage overcame their hesitation—seemingly minutes later, but not really—one of them managed to punch the doorbell.

"*Ahlan wa-sahlan,* you come as one of the family; may everything be smooth in your path. Do come in."

All smiles, the friendly, hospitable neighbors ushered their American visitors into the sitting room. Introductions were unnecessary; the whole neighborhood knew who Virginia and Nancie were. Everywhere they visited, it was the same: cordial conversation; questions back and forth. No, we don't celebrate this particular feast day in America. Yes, we both have families and we love them very much. Oh, yes, it's not uncommon for a young woman to be on her own in our country. Yes, we have feast days in the Baptist churches, I guess you could say. We do celebrate special occasions like Christmas and Easter.

Before long the family served sweet cakes prepared especially for the occasion. And hot coffee. Dark. Sweet. Poured, steaming, into small cups.

The husband brought small towels which both girls put on their laps. Nancie was delighted. She had been looking for a place to wipe her sticky fingers. Soon they took their leave, promising another visit soon.

Halfway down the stairs to the next floor, Virginia suggested that they had better go by their apartments.

"That's the last time," she said, "we go visiting wearing these tight skirts."

Nancie looked puzzled.

"You saw the man bring us towels?"

"Was I glad. My fingers were awful."

"Nancie, that's not why he brought the towels. Our short skirts, with nothing to cover our knees, offended the family."

Moving Publications

The move of Baptist Publications to its new home, the adjoining ground-floor apartments on Abu Haydar Street, was accomplished in early spring 1967. With major complications: illness and hospitalization for Virginia Cobb, and a noticeable deterioration in Arab-Western relationships due to the tense Arab-Israeli situation. However, the move did not precipitate the antagonisms anticipated by most of the publications staff. The lack of enthusiasm shown by Beirut Baptists continued. But none of the dire consequences predicted for the staff materialized.

At the new location, everybody was busy putting stock in order and trying to catch up on office routine. An inside door was cut behind the library room to give easy access to the office and storage space at the back of both apartments. Plans were drawn for bookstore and reading room shelving. Orders were placed for the stock of Arabic books, especially school texts, and supplies. The bookstore manager and others set up the inventory and sales procedures.

Meanwhile, as the correspondence course work grew, the main course, "The Life of Christ" (consisting of thirteen lessons, in workbook form), was in great demand. A second course, "The First Believers," based on the book of Acts, was offered to all who finished "The Life of Christ," and wanted more. All this spelled w-o-r-k for the staff, and necessitated a new staff position, the course grader. At first, an upperclassman at the Arab Baptist Theological Seminary filled this role.

Every time somebody wrote in about the course—perhaps in response to a newspaper ad or one of the radio programs—a carefully planned process was set in motion at Baptist Publications. First, send materials. Second, enter the person's name and other particulars, in the master file. With each first mailing, the opening lesson in "The Life of Christ" course, two individual Gospels (Mark and Luke), and a third Scripture portion (the Sermon on the Mount) were included.

With each subsequent lesson submitted, the course grader checked the correspondent's replies, making marginal notes. If specific questions were asked, the grader handled them, or turned to Miss Cobb for assistance.

As all of them worked in the new location, Marcelle Nasrallah, herself a Sunday School teacher, took time to get acquainted with the children who always played around the entrance to the building. One day, despite the fact that things were still in a jumble, Marcelle invited a little girl to come in and read a book if she liked.

Smiling, the child accepted. She was fascinated by what she saw, and full of questions about what the workmen were doing, and what was going to happen to all of the books stacked around wherever there was space for them.

"May I take one book home?" the girl asked.

Of course she could. Marcelle was careful to explain that she might keep the book five or six days, read it, and then return it.

Several days later the child was back—with a few friends who wanted to know if they, too, could borrow books.

Weathering a Storm

Soon, however, in May 1967, headlines screamed the deterioration of relations between the Arab countries and Israel. Radios blared loudly as partisans and patriots hurled charges and countercharges at each other. By the latter part of the month fighting seemed imminent. Some missionaries were evacuated from Gaza. The Foreign Mission Board assured all the Southern Baptist missionaries in the Middle East and North Africa to count on full backing for necessary emergency measures. The area secretary, Dr. J. D. Hughey, reminded them they were free to leave, or to remain, as seemed best. The experience of the Gaza missionaries alerted their colleagues to the gravity of the situation. Everybody was sensitive to local attitudes, because the missionaries knew that their presence could be a liability for national Christians.

Fighting began June 5. Only later was the designation, Six Day War, applied to the hostilities. Jordan missionaries, who had not felt they could leave, now found all airports and roads into their country closed. Lebanon, usually considered pro-Western, experienced serious anti-American demonstrations in Beirut.

Monday, June 5, was a day to be remembered. By the next afternoon, the missionaries in Beirut—in fact, all Americans there—were beginning to be apprehensive. Feeling was running high that the United States was "for" Israel and, therefore, "against" the Arabs. Tuesday afternoon the missionaries all received a message from the American Embassy: "Come immediately to the American University for processing."

The word that reached Nancie and Virginia, in their apartments in the Muslim quarter of the city, was the same: "Come now. Bring blankets. Bring food for twenty-four hours."

Both girls finished packing. Quickly. Reluctantly, really. They knew that they were—well, conspicuous.

"Where are you going?" a neighbor called from her balcony as they left the apartment building, suitcases in hand.

"Inshullah Tirjiauna, God willing, you shall return," another called.

"Allah Mykum, God go with you."

"Virginia, isn't it amazing how wonderful people can be to you personally, even when they feel your country is helping their enemy?"

By midnight the processing was finished and everybody was transferred to the airport. All but four of the Southern Baptist missionaries then in Lebanon were among the three thousand U.S. civilians evacuated by chartered flights. Nancie Wingo traveled on to the United States for a short furlough with her family in Texas. Virginia Cobb and other Southern Baptist missionaries from Beirut and Gaza were flown to Istanbul, and several days later to Rome. In six days the war was over. Within a few weeks most all of the missionaries were back in the Middle East.

But in the interim in Rome, Virginia became well known to the officials at the American Embassy. Daily she went there to ask one question: May I return to Beirut today?

Her colleagues had hoped that Virginia would accept the enforced stay in Rome as time for relaxation.

"Take a little vacation," they urged her. She needed it after the hectic months of moving the publications office, complicated by two periods of hospitalization and serious surgery within the year.

Vacation was not on Virginia's mind. She kept pestering the embassy. Kindly. Determinedly.

At first, return visas were granted only to businessmen. The next three, though, were issued to Virginia and two fellow missionaries, Mrs. J. Conrad Willmon and Mrs. James K. Ragland.

"Maybe it was a mistake," Jeannine Willmon said, "or luck—or more likely because of Virginia's determination; we don't know. But the Embassy granted us visas and we returned only eleven days after being evacuated; the first American women to return to Beirut."

"The airport is as sad as when I got here in '58," Virginia wrote to Nancie. "In fact, many things now are the same as then. Tensions. Fear. Tight security.

"I picked up your camera from the shop, and the manager was almost in mourning about the absence of tourists and foreign residents. 'When are the foreigners coming back?' he asked me. 'Lebanon is all very sad now. Times are hard.'"

Missionary James Ragland, one of those who had stayed in Beirut through the Six Day War, met Virginia with the news that her apartment had been looted.

Things were in disarray. Winter clothes were gone. Linens. Dishes. A green rug. A coffee table. The checkers and chessmen were missing but the rook cards had been left behind.

The intruders had written on the walls. "Long live Gamal Nasser." "Death to the spies of imperialism." But with second thoughts, they had drawn a line through this latter statement.

The record player and a typewriter were sitting beside the door, with a note of apology, in beautiful Arabic script:

> We beg your pardon. We thought you were engaged in political work against the Arab, but we noticed from books and letters that are present that you are engaged in religious matters and not in political matters. Therefore, we beg that you will forgive us.
> (signed) *Ikhwatukum,* your brethren

"It's good this happened," Virginia wrote to Nancie, "since it shows that they accept and respect a person who is concerned with religion only—even if not their religion. And now whoever it was, knows us in that capacity."

Much to the consternation of her colleagues, Virginia moved back into her apartment. The neighbors came to express regret and concern. "Forty houses around a man's home contain his neighbors," insists Islamic tradition. In typical Arab hospitableness, a man carries many responsibilities toward his neighbor: to visit him in sickness, to comfort him in trouble, to congratulate him on joyous occasions, to forgive his wrongs, and to watch over his house in his absence. Virginia's neighbors were no exception—without the provocation of war.

Virginia received her neighbors gladly. The landlady. The couple upstairs, with their baby. The people on the ground floor. The boys in the electrical shop. The mother of the family downstairs.

"And Nancie," she wrote, "I found enough of my stainless spoons and forks at your house to suffice. Fortunately, there were enough linens in the laundry to do me. I borrowed two plates from you, and the ironing board."

Building Relationships

Big padlocks were put on the door of the Baptist publications office during the evacuation period. Only the shipping foreman went in. But as soon as Virginia Cobb returned—the day after Muhammad's birthday—the staff returned to work and things soon returned to near normal. No new books were released during the summer, but several were pushed toward completion.

Older children came to know if they could borrow books. And high school students. Then university fellows and girls. The coffee bill went up (serving coffee in an Arab tradition of hospitality). Then the mothers, who first read what their children took home, themselves began coming. They wanted books on child care. And some of them wanted to talk about religion.

One woman, in particular, talked about God.

"God is the Creator," Virginia explained in response to a question. "Very great, yes; always present. But in his love there is a new relationship. God says, 'Come near.' God becomes our Father. God is interested in all of life, even the smallest details."

The two of them talked on more than one occasion.

"But I just never knew there were any Christians who believe what you do about a personal God."

The woman explained that she had not really talked with many Christians. Or ever attended a meeting of any congregation. She read some. She had heard reports about Christians now and then.

"I thought all of them were full of superstitions about saints and statues and priests."

She left with some books to read. Later she returned with more questions and to get more books. The people in the bookstore heard that she had defended the Christians to her neighbors. Several weeks later she came, hesitantly, with another question: "If I decide to believe in Christ, would I have to leave my husband and children?"

By the time school reopened that fall—1967—the Baptist Center was in full swing. All the carpentry had been finished. The bookstore shelves were stocked. The reading room was really ready to accommodate visitors.

Remembering the attitudes of the staff in the old office, Virginia felt that all of them were now willing to work hard and to wait as long as necessary to win the friendship of the people in the Muslim neighborhood. Already she was encouraged by people's response to Marcelle and to Mr. Hoshi, the book store manager. She was confident that this hope to win friendship was the serious aim of everybody connected with the center.

"Christian young people enjoyed coming to see us at the old location, Miss Cobb. We pray now that Muslim young people will come here."

Marcelle was concerned.

"I do like our new neighbors," she continued. "Maybe the older ones, and even adults, will follow the kids who are visiting us."

"Yes," Virginia smiled. "And even ask to read some Christian literature."

One day a group of university students came to Baptist Center. They talked with Mr. Hoshi and asked about the other people there. They were surprised to learn about the radio programs and the correspondence course. The map on the wall, with pins to represent places across the Arab world from which letters had come, was especially interesting.

"You mean you get letters from so many?" one asked.

"Yes," they said, explaining how people come to find out about the correspondence course, and something about the courses available.

The visitors walked back through the shipping room and into the literature storage area.

"Sunday School material?" one asked, examining some of the quarterlies.

"Sunday School," one of the staff told him, "is a Bible study program carried on in Baptist churches.

THE GIFT OF BELONGING
And other Christian groups have Sunday Schools too. In fact, almost everywhere you find Christians, you find Sunday Schools, and certainly serious Bible study."

Everybody was frank with the students. At first no one was sure whether they had come out of curiosity, or perhaps with hostile intent. They stayed a long time. They walked through all of the offices, just looking. They picked books off the shelves in the reading room, scanning some. Checking titles. Commenting to each other, and sometimes to the staff.

"So many books in Arabic!" one said. "I didn't really know that some of these were available in our language."

"One purpose in our publication work is to get books—good books—into Arabic," Mr. Hoshi told the student. "Biblical subjects, but also books of importance in many fields of thought. If we find a topic we feel needs to be covered in Arabic, and no other publisher has anything, we try to meet that need. Theology. Novels. Biography. Social subjects. We exist to serve people."

"You have English books, too," another student observed.

"Yes. Also some in French. A few in German. And most in Arabic." Mr. Hoshi was specific. "We also have some supplies that students may need. And textbooks."

The students' visit was friendly. The staff felt they had come because they really did want to find out about this new place in their neighborhood.

"No one in this area has ever tried to perform such

a service for us," one of the students said, as they prepared to leave.

"Or have anything on so high a moral level," another added.

"We do appreciate what you are doing."

The students left and the staff talked among themselves. Perhaps there *was* a place for a Christian bookstore and reading room in a Muslim community.

In the weeks following, Virginia and the staff were able to report high interest in their place, especially in the reading room. People continued to come. Young fellows like Hamid, who kept coming back and reading quite a few Christian novels.

"I don't know what you've done to me! I used to hate my neighbor and spend all my time reading filthy novels for sale on the street. Now I think you took away the old Hamid and brought in a new one! I like my neighbor, and I have no interest in those stories."

Hamid's friend, Abd Allah, told the staff that their store, and the reading room, had changed the whole neighborhood.

"We don't hear so much quarrelling and cursing on the street, and people are coming from blocks away just to read your books."

Abd Allah might have been exaggerating, but by the end of October it had become necessary to have "just certain hours" for book borrowing. It became necessary to have "days" for elementary pupils and other "days" for high school students. When someone expressed disappointment at the posting of hours, it was explained that the staff had other work which had to be done along with the operation of the lending library.

To the publications committee of the Arab Baptist Mission, Virginia reported 150 books borrowed in one week.

"The neighbors are now our fast friends, and the staff is convinced that showing Christ's love to Muslims is not only possible but a great joy.

"We have not yet completed the installations nor put up a sign in front," she concluded. "But God has already done 'more than we asked or thought.' We were willing to work slowly. But God did not wait."

Meanwhile in the Karantina

After the Six Day War, while the bookstore and reading room were taking shape in the Basta, a related development was underway in Karantina, the slum area of Beirut, of concern to some of the Baptist congregations in the city.

In the years since the first group visited in Karantina, in 1961, various approaches were tried. The Sunday afternoon Bible hours, with songs and stories, grew as the children learned to anticipate the event. Some of them never could sit still for a Bible story. But the church people who went grew accustomed to distractions. At least they discovered that the distractions were of more concern to them than to the Karantinians.

After the Baptists were able to move out of the two rooms they first rented in a tin-can shack, they obtained a small apartment with a balcony. Before too long the owner agreed to enclose the balcony to make it usable even in the winter. That helped the space problem some.

Among themselves the missionaries were now talking about expanding the work in Karantina. They envisioned a goodwill center-type ministry with a full weekday program of activities. As it was, five groups met weekly, and were reaching about two hundred children and youth under seventeen.

Naturally, with Virginia Cobb and others in publication and school work related to Karantina, somebody had to suggest a library there.

"So many books!"

"What do you do with a book?"

The first time the Karantina young people saw "their library" they were puzzled. They watched Virginia come time after time, carting in books for the library. With the help of some of the others, a checkout desk was improvised, and the library explained to the youngsters.

"Yes, you may take a book home with you. And when you bring that book back you may borrow another one."

Some of the books were much worse for the wear. A few never did get back. More than once a strange bulge under a ragged dress would call attention to a hidden book. Some books were stolen—the Bible more than any other.

Those in charge of the library watched how hard it was for the children to decide which book to take home. It was commonplace for a child to decide to take a book home and start toward the checkout desk, only to go back and look over the bookshelf another time. Even at the checkout desk, more than one would change his mind again.

"The poor have so few choices," Jeannine Willmon observed. And the Karantina library taught the Christians who worked there how agonizing one choice can be.

Understanding and loving the Karantinians, Virginia Cobb was patient with them when "her" books got rough treatment. She rebound the books. Sometimes she replaced them. Every week she spent time in the library, talking with those who came, sharing her love for books, encouraging this one, or that, in a conversation beginning with some book that the child was interested in.

For a while Jeannine Willmon and Virginia worked together with one of the weekday afternoon groups in Karantina. When one of the members was to be married, they planned a party. The honoree, Nabiha by name, was frank to say she did not want to marry the young man her family had chosen. But, like a good Muslim bride-to-be, she expected to go along with the wedding plans.

"We were trying our best to help her," Jeannine explained. "We wanted to make her as happy as possible, and hoped we could teach the whole group something about the sanctity and festivity of marriage."

At one club meeting, a party was announced for the next club meeting. Jeannine planned games, especially one she thought would be just right. She fixed four envelopes and filled each with the same amount of the same materials: paper, rubber bands, scotch tape, toothpicks, scissors, glue.

When everything was arranged in the meeting, Jeannine divided the girls into four groups and promised a prize for the group making the nicest house for Nabiha.

Nobody did anything. Not one group opened their envelope of materials. Jeannine explained it all again.

"This is a game—a fun thing—to build a house for Nabiha. Open your envelope and use all the materials you find there. Okay, let's get to work. The group that makes Nabiha the finest house gets a prize."

Nobody made a move to use the materials.

Jeannine looked at Virginia. "I'm not doing well with Arabic; will you please explain the idea again?"

"There's nothing wrong with your Arabic." Virginia smiled, and then made the explanation with step-by-step detail. "You open the envelope," she said, "and lay out all of the materials."

Then, item by item, Virginia gave the girls instructions which they followed to the letter, giggling and enjoying every minute of it.

Jeannine learned just how stifled a person's creative instinct can become in the čircumstances familiar in the difficult life of the Karantinians.

"It's just hard to imagine how people feel when they have never had anything to work with," Virginia told Jeannine.

The whole point of all the Baptist effort in the Karantina was to give new opportunities to people with so little. For those lucky enough to be in school, the Baptist young people and some of the missionaries provided tutoring—in geometry, algebra, English, or whatever help they needed. The project is old enough now that some who began to come as ragged street urchins too young for school, now anticipate graduation. What the future holds for them is hard to say, but the fact that they continue to attend classes and club meetings speaks their appreciation for Christian friends who care.

Daily Encounters

When Nancie Wingo returned from her short furlough during the summer of the Six Day War, she and Virginia found a fourth-floor apartment a few buildings down from the Baptist Center and on the other side of the street.

There was an electrical shop on the first floor, and also a grocery store. There were other shops close by: a tailor, a radio repair shop, and a variety store. They were close enough to the mosque next door to the Saudi Center (the Muslim meeting hall) to hear the daily prayer calls. In fact, as they learned later, the muezzin—the man who gave the prayer calls five times daily—lived in their block. Despite their being Americans, and Christians, Nancie and Virginia experienced friendship in the Muslim neighborhood. Actually, everyone was overwhelmingly open. People often stopped Virginia on the street just to talk. The other residents in the apartment building were most friendly. The schoolteacher in the apartment above them, and the family across the hall with eight children. When Virginia and Nancie first moved in, the apartment next door was vacant. When it was rented, imagine their joy to discover that their new neighbors were newlyweds, and that the bride was a graduate of Beirut Baptist School.

The friendly neighbors just upstairs over the bookstore and reading room itself, were devout Muslims, but quite interested in these Christians who had come to work in their midst. When the office staff was moving in, this family brought down coffee for everybody.

The two missionaries continued their efforts to get to know the neighbors and to be known by them. The mother above the Baptist Center was particularly interesting to talk with. All this family took their religion seriously, as evidenced by the mother's veil, a custom now increasingly uncommon in cosmopolitan Beirut, and in the rest of the Arab world.

During one feast day visit, this gracious woman told Nancie and Virginia that she had lived near some Christians once before, when she was first married.

"I loved those people," she said. "My faith teaches me, as one who loves God, to love others who also love God."

She talked about the children in their family, so proud that at least one son was studying to become a religious leader.

During school vacations, this young man was a frequent visitor in the reading room. He learned about the correspondence course, "The Life of Christ," and completed it himself. He began reading the New Testament. In one of the novels he checked out to read, he found the quotation, "In all these things we are more than conquerors through him that loved us."

"Where is this quotation found?" he asked.

Later a Muslim woman, despairing, asked this young man to teach her something about faith.

Instead, he came to the reading room with this request: "Please write down for me some verses on the peace and joy that Christ offers. Why should

I tell this woman of our religion when Christianity offers this victory?"

Virginia was at home with these people. She and Nancie knew many of them by name. In their daily rounds they often greeted the old sheik who ran a small barber shop. Virginia often stopped to chat with a bookbinder in the neighborhood, a sincerely religious man, who enjoyed discussing his faith.

"I serve God doing a good job of bookbinding," he often told her, "and you, Miss Cobb, are serving God, too, in the work you do.

"Where else can people in this community find the services your center provides? If a student needs a textbook, or some writing supplies, your center is open. I say it's good. Very good."

For several blocks in any direction, no other store in the community carried Christian books. In addition, the reading room provided an informal meeting place. A study hall, really. Few of the modest homes in the neighborhood could boast many books or magazines. And on the whole, the community provided few recreational opportunities. But Baptist Center quickly became *the* place to go. It was a meeting place that provided opportunities to see other young people and freedom for conversation. Most important, perhaps, there were interested persons willing to take time to talk. Frequently the conversations deepened into honest dialogue about spiritual matters.

All the next summer, after the war, the reading room was used by students preparing for government examinations. When the reading room proper filled up, the young people looked for other quiet spots around the premises: the backyard, the kitchen, a corner in the bookstore—even back in the stockroom.

Despite their increasing work load, the staff still found time to be helpful and friendly. They discovered that many students willingly brought them questions about religion. And to direct inquiries, they did not hesitate to bear witness to their faith, being careful not to criticize Islam as they talked.

Two months during the summer special activities were offered. A beginner's class in English met three times a week. After it began, this class had to be divided into two sessions to meet the demand for this level of instruction. Two advanced English classes were also offered and, later, a music class.

Twice a week "book days," set aside for returning borrowed ones and checking out new books, were extremely busy. Nobody could miss the young people crowding the sidewalk around the center waiting their turn to get in. Talking. Laughing. Enjoying each other's company.

A check of the card file showed more than 1,600 borrower's cards in circulation. So many, in fact, that plans were made to issue a series of cards with perhaps a small fee.

Periodically all the books were called in for checking and repair. The inventory for the first full year showed wide circulation of all the books available, with 148 lost—or worn out. The records confirmed Miss Cobb's feeling that people outside the churches were not likely to select a Bible study book or a sermon collection.

For this reason, the publications department of the Mission included novels, biographies, and other literary forms in its translation-publishing schedule.

Interestingly, the missionary biography, *Bill Wallace of China*, was well received in the Arabic-language edition. One report on this title came from a post office official who was given a copy by the Baptist Publications' shipping clerk.

"I stayed up all night reading this book. Please tell me more about what you believe," he wrote in his letter.

A small book on existentialism met unexpected popularity.

"There is great interest in this subject by secular publishers," Virginia said, "and this brief treatment from the Christian viewpoint speaks to present-day concerns."

All the while, the Baptist Center staff was involved in handling the correspondence courses, the response to radio programming, and the curriculum materials for the churches and schools.

Meeting Opposition

Over breakfast, just after New Year's Day, 1968, Virginia was talking with Nancie about what had happened in their venture of understanding.

"When we first talked about moving publications over here, Nancie, I thought about the Christian young people who were visiting the old office." Smearing toast with a generous knife-full of jam, she kept on talking.

"They asked for books, and I thought, well, if we go into a Muslim neighborhood, maybe after they get to know us, and become our friends, just maybe, Muslim young people will ask to read Christian literature."

"But we never dreamed so many would come, huh?"

"I hoped for a few," Virginia admitted, "but God's expectations were so much greater than mine."

Turning around to the stove, Virginia refilled both coffee cups.

"I thought that little by little we'd be able to build up this work, as we made friends in the neighborhood."

The morning sun, already high, reminded the girls that despite the luxury of an occasional free morning, there was work to do. A new school term about to begin for Nancie. A year-end report due Virginia's publications committee. And by the sounds from outside, another day had long ago begun in the Basta.

The pastry vendor and the kerosene man were on their rounds. The plastics seller was calling attention to his products. The vegetable man had opened up his cart and already some of the housewives in the apartment building were haggling over the cost of fresh produce.

Nancie cleared the table.

"We'll have to say that Baptist Center has been doing something to the status quo around here.

"The young people are saying, 'This is *our* reading room,' Virginia said thoughtfully.

"That's because they know us." Nancie reached for the tea kettle to rinse the dishes she had stacked on the sink.

"They know what we believe. They know we care for them as persons," Virginia said. "But the results we must leave to God."

That spring most of the Baptist missionaries in Beirut left the city one weekend for a retreat. When they returned, they found that someone had stolen the sign in front of Baptist Center. A note was left to the effect that they—whoever "they" were—did not like "American-Jewish evangelists." A few months later an attempt was made to set fire to the building. Kerosene was thrown against the shutters on the front of the Center and then ignited. Damage was slight, but the incident caused concern. Efforts were made to seek police protection, and to secure insurance benefits for the people living in the apartments above Baptist Center.

This opposition, when it came, was in contrast to the community openness which had surprised everyone connected with Baptist Center.

"We expected that when we moved in people would ask 'why are you here? what are you doing?'" Virginia recalled. "We anticipated that some in the neighborhood would resent our presence. We were prepared to work quietly, patiently to win friendship. But instead, we found response and friendliness from the beginning.

"Should we really be surprised to meet some opposition?"

The surprising thing was that the open opposition was so long in coming. The violence of the attempt to burn the Center was a serious matter not only for the staff, but for the Baptists in Beirut, and for the whole neighborhood. Gradually things returned to normal. At least on the surface the community was calm. People still came to Baptist Center in large numbers. The young people still studied there. The staff continued to respond with friendship and help-fulness.

Then, after the first of the year, 1969, some of the young people began to bring to the Center reports that new violence was being planned. In the schools and in the mosque, some said, it was being suggested that they should stay away from the Baptist Center.

The situation remained tense. Young people, discussing the matter with their friends at the Center, suggested that Miss Cobb visit the sheik in charge of the nearby mosque.

"There may be some misunderstanding," they said. "They can't do this to *our* reading room."

Several of the young people took Miss Cobb, and Missionary Emmett Barnes, to visit the sheik.

"The sheik was understanding of our purposes," Virginia said later. "And the next Friday, in his sermon at the mosque, he said that all people must live together in the neighborhood."

Problems were not limited to the neighborhood.

Lebanon was politically uncertain about itself all through the decade of the sixties. Between the 1958 revolution and the Six Day War in 1967, many problems surfaced. Being half-Christian and half-Muslim, Lebanon continued to be plagued by many opposing views. Many people were concerned to try to maintain a balance in government. In the face of the Palestinian problem, and the proximity of Lebanon's southern mountain area to Israel, many voices were heard. Before mid-year 1969, the country was actually without any official government at all, a situation that lasted many days.

All of these social and political realities were felt

in the Basta. Being a Muslim community, the hope for solidarity had to be sought in Islamic traditions. At least, collectively, most people thought so. In these circumstances it was natural that the opposition to Baptist Center, now that it had surfaced, would come to the attention of persons in official positions in Beirut. These men were charged with the responsibility of maintaining a viable situation for every community in the city.

About a week after the "we-must-live-together" sermon at the mosque, Virginia was called to a government office. She was interviewed by an official who asked one question: "Why did you come into this neighborhood?"

"We came," Virginia told the official, "because Christians and Muslims should not live with prejudice and misunderstanding between them. We ought to be able to live together. We think there should be friendship and understanding. So our purpose is a first move in this direction. We moved into the Muslim neighborhood to serve the community."

"A good motive. I like it. You should stay. I will talk with the sheik."

The visit was brief, but the official was understanding. He explained to Virginia that there are people who cannot appreciate such efforts to break down prejudice.

"If we are forced to close, sir, it will be taken as proof that what the Christians told us when we moved in is true, namely, that Christians and Muslims cannot work together. But, sir, I do not believe this is true."

"Let's see if you can keep working without any more trouble," the official said.

Some days later the official came to Baptist Center. He wanted to see for himself what facilities and services were available. After his inspection, he thanked the staff and left wishing them God's blessings.

In early May, however, the government official sent for Virginia a second time.

This interview began by recalling the pleasant impressions of his visit to the Center. Then he explained that those who bear responsibility for the security and peace of Lebanon felt now that the bookstore and reading room could no longer stay in its present location.

"We want to serve," Virginia responded. "We do believe there can be understanding and friendship between Christians and Muslims, but if our staying hinders this, then, of course, we will not stay."

The official was firm.

So Monday, May 12, 1969, as people brought books back to the reading room, the staff explained that no more books could be borrowed at present.

"Yes, we will let you know where we relocate the reading room."

"If you move to another neighborhood, we will follow you," some said.

"To the moon, or anywhere on earth!" one fellow added.

Many expressed regret.

An elderly woman who accompanied some young children to the Center was hard pressed to understand Miss Cobb's explanation of why the book-borrowing had to stop.

"May *Allah* open their hearts," she said sadly.

"I think these people really will come to the reading room outside this neighborhood," Virginia told Nancie as they watched the woman leave. "But what if we hadn't come here first?"

"Do you know why you have all this trouble?" one friend, himself a municipal official, asked. "Because you have a message. Muhammad had a message. They persecuted him, and put thorns in his way. If you didn't have persecution, it would mean that you weren't presenting a message.

A message.

The message!

As far as Virginia Cobb was concerned, the message about who Christ is was all there was. And she believed that people would understand the message best if they could see it walking around in their neighborhood.

قد فارقت وحنايا الغرب تحويها

بلوعـة ، ومـآق الشرق تبكيها

وطيفهـا في السحاب الهف ودعنا

بسمة عذبة فاضت على فيهـا

احل لقد قصف الاعصار زهرتنا

امامنـا بينما بالدمــع نرويها

اجل لقد صعق الجبار نعجتنـا

ما بيننا بينما في الصدر نحميها

صفحا ايا ربنا في ظرفنـا ان تكن

قلوبنا استسلمت للحزن يكويها

عفوا لاشجاننا في خطبنا ان نكن

رجاؤنا قد توارى في حواشيها

ينتابنا خجل لذكرنا كيف قــد

كانت شجاعتها في الهول تبديها

اذاكر عندمـا ذاك الخبيث اتى

اعراضه في نحيل الجسم يرسيها

وعادها الكل مذهولـين وازدحمت

رحابهـا بجموع من محبيهـا

وغصة اسكت تلك الجموع واذ

هي التي بالرجا كانت تعزيهـا

وكم وكم من مزايا سوف نذكرها

اذا اردنـا لها ذكرى نحييها

هي التي غادرت اوطانهـا ونأت

من بعد ان فارقت فيها اهاليها

وشمرت عـن ذراع الكـد واندفعت

بغيرة خدمـة للرب فادبهـا

مـا غرها ما احتوت بيروت من نعم

ما هزها ما ازدهت بذخا علاليها

وكان ان انت يومـا جئت تطلبها

ففي زوايـا الكرنتينـا تلاقيها

IN MEMORY OF VIRGINIA COBB
by Bassam Afeish

كم قاصر شجعت ٠ كم عاجز ساندت

كم من عجوز انت بالسر تعطيها

تلك البساطة في شخصية زادها

من نيّر العقل الوان توشيها

آراؤهـــا حجة كانت لنـا ولكم

نصائح للذي قد حار تسديهـا

قد اتقنت لغة الاعراب بـــل انهـا

توغلت بفلاح فـــي فيافيهـا

وانشأت لبــلاد الشرق مكتبـــة

روحيـــة فتجد مهما ترد فـها

سدت فراغا لدينا واسعا فلـــذا

اولى بنا بلسان الضاد نرثيهـا

فرجينا يا ملاكـــا حل في ارضنا

هنيهة واختفى من بين اهليهـا

يظل ذكرك حيا فـــي مرابعنـا

ما ضوعت من شذى عطر اقاحيها

تريدنـي ان اوفي اختنا حقهـا

من الرثاء وان احصي مآتيهـا

هيهات هيهــات ان احظى بما ابتغي

من ذا الذي يدعي حقــا يوفبهـا

يكفي لهــا ان اجيالا ترى واذا

خلال آثارهــا من نبل ماضيها

على المدى داخل التاريخ قلـب روى :

$+ ٢٠٧ + ١٣٢$

قرب الحبيب عن الامجاد يغنيها

$٣٠٢ + ٥٣ + ١٢٠ + ٨٠ + ١٠٧٦$

$= ١٩٧٠$

بسام عفيش

**(English translation of this poem appears on the fol-
lowing page.)**

134

She left her country and her family and came to faraway lands.

She rolled up her sleeves and stretched forth her working arm and poured out herself in service to her Lord.

She was never tempted or fascinated by luxury; nothing attracted her in the pompous city of Beirut.

If you looked for her, you would find her in the corners of the slums of Karantina. Oh, how many children she encouraged! How many incapacitated ones she helped secretly!

She was so simple but her broad and brilliant mind adorned her person. Her opinions were authentic. Her advice was bestowed upon those who were stricken by dilemma and perplexity.

She mastered the language of the Arabs and traveled far and deep into its deserts very successfully.

She established a great spiritual library in the East where you can find a book on any subject you desire.

She filled a great gap; therefore, we are the first to mourn her in our beautiful Arabic language.

EPILOGUE

EPILOGUE

Late June, 1969—two months after the bookstore and reading room were closed—I asked Missionary Virginia Cobb why. As we sat in her office in the Baptist Center, it was hard to believe that this warm, friendly place was a trouble spot. Sunshine streamed through an open door. Virginia had just finished a meeting with her staff and they had gone back to the work of packing up books from the reading-room shelves.

"Look at it this way," Virginia explained. "How would *you* feel if a group of Muslims came into *your* community and started attracting young people in large numbers?"

With disarming winsomeness, Virginia had done just that. With the backing of the publications committee of the Arab Baptist General Mission, she had moved into the Basta, a Muslim community in Beirut, to spearhead a program so compelling that, in retrospect, it is probably fair to say the reading room was too successful.

"But now," she continued, "a few people see that the project was feasible and, in fact, has borne fruit."

"What did you hope to accomplish?"

"We wanted to get into the Basta," Virginia told me, "because the national churches were not trying to bridge this misunderstanding between Christians and Muslims. We felt that by moving into the neighborhood we could make contact with people."

Virginia paused a moment.

"I think God called me here," she said softly. "Christ is concerned for these people. He came for them as much as for anyone else. I think there is great hope that Muslims will respond to Christ."

A year after its closing, the Baptist bookstore and reading room in Beirut reopened within easy walking distance of the old location in the Basta. The new site meets the requirements of those who wanted the Baptist complex moved out of the Muslim community. It is in a new building on the right-of-way for a proposed four-lane thoroughfare to downtown Beirut. In addition, it affords easy access to the post office, the printers, and supply stores important to any publication work.

There is, of course, one major difference. The Baptist Center in Beirut no longer has the services of Mary Virginia Cobb. On January 25, 1970, in Statesboro, Georgia, she died, succumbing to the cancer that first attacked her body before the move to the Basta.

Her successor as director of Baptist publication work is a missionary colleague, Frances (Mrs. J. Wayne) Fuller.

Just after New Year's Day 1972, Frances Fuller and the others at Baptist Publications received from the printer a new book in Arabic, *The Heart of the Bible.* This book is actually a "condensed Bible" especially suitable for someone who has never read the Bible, or for a child. The initial printing of 5,000 copies was given to persons enrolling in the correspondence courses available from Baptist Publications.

Publication costs were defrayed by the Virginia Cobb Memorial Fund—a gift from her home church, First Baptist Church, Statesboro, Georgia.

"The Heart of the Bible is a perfectly appropriate and memorable project for the Statesboro gift," Mrs. Fuller wrote to the congregation, "because this book was born in Virginia's mind. I am simply tending a plant which I found already growing."

During the final editing of the book, Frances found a note Virginia had scribbled on the back of a letter to clarify a point about the book which someone coming after her would need to know.

"When I read that note," Frances continued to the Statesboro people, "I felt sure she knew she would not finish this job but trusted someone would.

"Virginia loved the correspondence course and received obvious joy from every response to it. We felt that you would like nothing better than to provide Bibles for hundreds, hopefully thousands, of people who would not otherwise have one. Let us pray that what we have done together will lengthen the witness of Virginia Cobb and bring glory to the Savior."

AN APPROACH TO WITNESS

AN APPROACH TO WITNESS

Late June and early July 1969, a group of Southern Baptist missionaries held a week-long conference in Teheran, Iran. They were representatives of the various Missions (organizations of missionaries within a given country) in the Middle East. They came together to focus attention upon their primary task; namely, Christian witness among Muslims. They considered the Christian message, and effective methods of missionary work.

In preparation for Teheran, a series of papers were written in the Missions. The Lebanon Mission, asked to prepare a paper on missionary methods for work among Muslims, turned to a member of the group— Virginia Cobb, who was also asked to be one of Lebanon's representatives to the conference.

Detained in Beirut by illness, Virginia did not reach Teheran until after her paper had been read by a fellow missionary, J. W. (Bill) Trimble. By conference consensus, her "Missionary Methods for Work Among Muslims" was named *the* paper of the conference, and the hope was expressed that it could be given wide circulation among Baptists and other Christians.

Virginia's paper was printed in *The Commission*, the Southern Baptist Foreign Mission Journal, September

THE GIFT OF BELONGING

1970, under the title, "An Approach to Witness." Four months later it was reprinted in German translation in *Die Gemeinde,* the publication of the German Baptist Union, with this comment: "Basic in missionary theory and method."

Often where we have no answer, we can have an attitude that will lead us as we search for the answers. This is the view of Dr. Kenneth Cragg, a missionary teacher and writer.

What should be our attitude as Christians toward Muslims?

ATTITUDE

We are not warring with Islam. If we were, we couldn't afford to give any quarter, to let anything go unchallenged, to admit any good or truth. We would be happy to damage it as much as possible, to show every weakness or inconsistency. But this is contrary to the spirit of Christ. And a major error in any struggle is to pursue the wrong enemy. Our enemy is evil, God's enemy. Islam teaches love of God, supreme loyalty to him, great reverence, and high principles of character.

One strong criticism of Christian missions has been that they have destroyed men's faith in Islam without winning those men to Christ, leaving them worse off. It cannot be God's will that we leave men in worse condition than we found them! And it should not be necessary. A sincere Muslim is nearer to God and to Christ than a man with no faith. Christianity, like

Islam, has produced wars, persecutions, bigotry, and empty forms; we do not, therefore, war against it but seek a truer understanding of it.

We are not debating with Islam to prove that our views are correct and theirs incorrect. Were we, we might rely on polemics, logical proofs, etc. But no one is won by this method or convinced against his will. This approach makes the basic mistake of acting as if Christian faith were credence rather than commitment to a Person, an act of the intellect rather than of the whole person. It ignores the fact that our doctrines came about as an attempt to explain in comprehensible terms our experience, ie., they follow, rather than precede, experience.

We are not trying to change anyone's religion. Religion consists of affiliation with a group, cult, ethic, orthodoxy. The New Testament is quite clear that none of these saves. It is possible to change all of them without knowing God. If we stress these, we may give the impression that these things *are* the Christian faith.

Our attitude should be one of love and acceptance. God accepts and loves them as they are. He is already reconciled to them, "not counting their trespasses against them." If we, the ministers of his reconciliation, are "reconciled" to them, we will accept them as persons as able as ourselves and as deserving of respect and a hearing of their views. We will not go to straighten them out or tell them all the answers. If we are reconciled to them, we will be able to appreciate all that is true, good, commendable, and worthy in their lives as individuals and in their culture and religion.

We need stronger *faith in the power of the truth*. It is in no danger from the fullest, best possible expression of contrary views, from the teaching of the Qur'an [Koran], or from comparison, scrutiny, or the honest admission of the failures of historic Christianity or of Christian people. Nor is it in danger if we forego the temptation to defend the nonessential, secondary parts of our beliefs and practices in order to keep the door open for discussion and emphasis on the (very few) essentials. Our insecurity and defensive attitude only hinder.

We need faith stronger in the reality of the living Christ. Everything does not depend on us. We do not have to present and gain assent to a complete system of theology and ethic. Some early disciples were content to say: Come and see. If we introduce them to a living Person, he will draw them, reveal himself to them, and teach them directly.

CONTACT

Identification. Christ, in his incarnation, came to dwell in the midst of those he came to save, and became like them in everything but sin. This meant a full entering into the life of the people. It meant speaking their language, using terms and concepts they understood, dealing with problems they faced and values they held.

This principle cannot be applied by setting up a meeting place and inviting people to come. It cannot be applied by living in relative isolation from them, in a separate quarter, or with little day-to-day contact. It cannot be applied by using the terminology Christians have grown accustomed to and others do not know (Holy Spirit, rebirth, etc.).

It means close association, sharing in everything possible, and an awareness of their concerns, problems, hopes, value system. Speaking their language means not just grammar and syntax, but studying their culture and religion to learn the terms and values they comprehend.

Love. Christ's love was a genuine concern for the total welfare of those he came to save. It was demonstrated, not spoken. It was not limited to salvation from judgment, but included healing, moral teaching, crossing social barriers, comforting, calming, freeing, touching the untouchables, and befriending sinners. He did these things not merely as bait, but in many instances where no mention is made of "evangelism."

To love as he did means seeking the good of others in every sphere, actively and without reciprocation, even without appreciation, without conversions. It means accepting the inconvenience or hurt they may cause us without lessening our positive efforts on their behalf. Perhaps the only way we can prove—to ourselves and others—that we love in this way is to be really concerned about the "this-worldly" welfare of some who reject the message, to feel real friendship for some outside the circle of believers, to keep on serving those we feel will not be won.

How can we expect a Muslim to accept a bare statement of a belief so different, against which he is already conditioned, with no demonstration of its power or meaning? What would be required to make *you* give serious consideration to another religion? God won us by coming to us and outloving our enmity. We can only present his gospel by going to them and outloving their suspicion, enmity, and rejection.

Therefore, there must be *some concrete demonstration of love.* It can be personal, in the relationship between friends, or institutional—schools, hospitals, English classes, reading rooms, community centers (manned by the right persons), radio programs, and publications that are directed to real human needs.

We have seen in two different types of Muslim neighborhoods in Beirut that community service projects will draw overwhelming numbers, open to friendship and understanding, willing to listen to whatever is said tactfully. The services rendered must be a sincere expression of concern, *with no other motive.* Active, unselfish service in the name of Christ is more likely to win converts than zealous "preaching for results" which often turns persons away.

Law of reciprocity. Jesus clearly taught that we are in some measure able to control, and therefore, responsible for, the type response we elicit (Luke 6:37-38). If we give genuine friendship, openness to all that is good, respect and sensitivity for all that is dear to others, we may expect the same. If we go with closed minds, rejection of their ideas, suspicion, fear, or superiority, we may expect the same. If we refuse to listen in the truest sense, can we expect them to listen?

The example of our attitude toward Islam may set the pattern for their attitude toward Christianity.

RAPPORT

Here *attitude is all-important.* For if we make contact or have Muslims in our institutions or services, and then show an attitude of superiority or condemnation or enmity, or show disrespect to what is sacred to them, we not only lose them but create further animosity. Our relationship with them should be such as to inspire confidence in our sincere desire to serve them, our fair-mindedness, sensitivity, and appreciation of all that is good.

We should emphasize every point of agreement, encourage every true direction, praise all that is praiseworthy, put the best possible interpretation on every teaching or practice.

Our message is a Person we've experienced, not a doctrine, system, religion, book, church, ethic.

Christ is extremely attractive to Muslims. They have the highest respect for him and yearn to know more about him. We can present the person Jesus and his teachings as our supreme and only emphasis, the only thing we have to add to the foundation of reverence for God and moral emphasis already found in Islam.

Our faith in him is that once we lead a person to him, he will, in direct contact with that person, transform and guide in all else.

What of doctrines related to Christ himself? Jesus didn't insist on a certain view of himself as prerequisite to discipleship. He called men to follow him unconditionally and after two years of living with them asked what their conclusion was. He used the same method of induction with John the Baptist.

It is safe to leave people to draw their own conclusions after sincerely seeking to know Christ and experience him.

"Seek ye first the kingdom" means that all else

can be and must be sacrificed for the highest goal. We have many valued truths and emphases that may have to be left out of our efforts with others until long after they have come to know Christ for themselves, "laying upon them no greater burden than these necessary things" (Acts 15:28).

Many of our institutional forms as well as the details of doctrine hinder more than they help people coming from a different way of life, while Christ and his teachings attract with power. We must lay aside the weight of nonessentials for the sake of the essential.

DECISION

Christ presented the truth, the call, but never persuaded. He let men come to decision in personal freedom, and even discouraged some who misunderstood what was involved. We teach the competence and responsibility of each individual and, therefore, must urge every person to do only and exactly what he is convinced in his own heart he must do. We can only emphasize his responsibility before God to obey his best light. If he feels he should be a more faithful Muslim, we should encourage him to do so to the best of his ability, and to try to understand what it means in the fullest sense. If he feels he should try to follow Christ's teachings, we should encourage that, and wait until he feels the need for something more. When he feels he should commit himself to Christ regardless of the cost, we should encourage that, and stand by him in facing the dangers that may follow.

The convert and the seeker need real fellowship.

They have severe "culture shock" and need dependable, understanding friends. Since the national churches, at present, are very slow to provide this, and the Muslim often remains a relative outsider even if baptized, there may need to be other arrangements for fellowship—small groups or personal contacts.

Some converts may feel they can do more good by remaining within their own community, although in informal contact and fellowship with Christians. Jesus called no one to leave Judaism, and the first Christians remained in synagogue and Temple for some time. Our responsibility is to maintain the ties of fellowship and personal support.

Who? The national believers are now showing a little more interest in reaching non-Christians. However, their attitude is usually more likely to alienate than win. Therefore, we must take the lead in the approach described here, even in opposition to national Christian opinion.

However, a secondary aim and effect of our ministry to Muslims will be in helping national believers overcome prejudice by personal acquaintance with others. When they really know some Muslims, many are wise enough and kind enough to change those things in their approach and attitude that offend. They will then develop their own methods of presenting Christ to Muslims.

RESULTS

The effectiveness of the truth and the drawing power of Christ are sufficient to guarantee that some will be won in these ways. However, we have centuries of Christian enmity and harshness and rejection of Islam to atone for and undo; we have walls of prejudice built up through the centuries to break down; we have deeply ingrained attitudes in both Christians and Muslims to change.

Many years of friendship, love, service, without reciprocation and without much fruit, may be required before there exists a better atmosphere for the open sharing of views and open commitment to Christ. We must be willing to pay this price also.

SUMMARY

We must have an attitude of love and acceptance, and strong faith in the power of truth.

We must get into the midst of people, identify with them, and love them in deed, not word, in some concrete ways.

We must emphasize Christ as a living person, and leave all else in a secondary position.

We must talk openly, freely, and respectfully of religious matters, whether in regard to our religion or theirs, and emphasize the responsibility of the individual to God, to act according to his own best light.

We must do these things patiently for many years, regardless of the immediate results.